Jesus and Caesar

Jesus and Caesar

Christians in the Public Square

Brian C. Stiller

Foreword by Preston Manning

CASTLE QUAY BOOKS
CANADA

Jesus and Caesar: Christians in the Public Square
Copyright © 2003 by Castle Quay Books Canada
All rights reserved.
Printed in Canada
International Standard Book Number: 1-894860-04-7

Published by:
Castle Quay Books
1740 Pilgrim's Way, Oakville, Ontario, L6M 1S5
Tel: (416) 573-3249   Fax (519) 748-9835
E-mail: *info@castlequaybooks.com*
www.castlequaybooks.com

Cover Design by John Cowie, *eyetoeye, design*
Copy editing by Janet Dimond
Printed at Essence Publishing, Belleville, Ontario

Scripture quotations, unless otherwise indicated, are from the New International Version of the Bible, copyright ©1973, 1978 by the International Bible Society. Used by permission of Zondervan Publishers.

Scripture quotations marked KJV are from *The Holy Bible, King James Version,* copyright © 1977, 1984 Thomas Nelson Inc., Publishers.

Scripture quotations marked NASB are taken from the *New American Standard Bible*, copyright © The Lockman Foundation 1960, 1962, 1963, 1968, 1971, 1972, 1973. All rights reserved.

National Library of Canada Cataloguing in Publication

Stiller, Brian C.

Jesus and Caesar : Christians in the public square / Brian C. Stiller.

Includes bibliographical references and index.
ISBN 1-894860-04-7

1. Christianity and politics. I. Title.

BR115.P7S75 2003   261.7   C2002-906124-5

In dedication to the Honorable Jake Epp, colleague, friend, and Christian, who has modeled the integration of faith with spiritual well-being in the most challenging of environments, the world of politics and business.

Table of Contents

Foreword

D r. Brian C. Stiller, now the President of Tyndale College &
Seminary in Toronto, was also the President of the Evangelical
Fellowship of Canada from 1983 to 1997.

During this key period, when many evangelicals in the United
States were seeking to influence the politics of their country through
the Moral Majority movement, Stiller counselled Canadian
Christians to follow a "kinder, gentler path" and to seize the unique
opportunities for Christian witness which Canadian cultural pluralism provides.

Although he personally comes from a spiritual tradition which,
until recently, favoured withdrawal from the political world, in *Jesus
and Caesar*, Stiller counsels engagement. But he counsels Christians to
be engaged, not out of a dogmatic desire to impose our will on others, but with grace and wisdom.

In chapter 6 of *Jesus and Caesar*, Stiller quotes the following words
of Church of England pastor and teacher John Stott: "in social action
… we should neither try to impose Christian standards by force on an
unwilling public, nor remain silent and inactive before the contemporary landslide, nor rely exclusively on the dogmatic assertion of biblical values, but rather reason with people about the benefits of
Christian morality, commending God's law to them by rational arguments. We believe that God's laws are both good in themselves and

universal in their application because, far from being arbitrary, they fit the human beings God has made."

In each chapter of *Jesus and Caesar*, Stiller provides information and arguments which will assist Christians the world over to serve as salt and light in the societies and circumstances where God has placed them. Such information and arguments should also better enable us to practise the communication of our faith with "the wisdom of serpents and the harmlessness of doves" which our Lord commanded us to exhibit.

Stiller has rendered all of us a great service in setting out his views on how Christians ought to conduct themselves in the public square in the twenty-first century.

Preston Manning

Preface

The sea of faith
Was once, too, at the full, and round earth's shore
Lay like the folds of a bright girdle furl'd;
But now I only hear
Its melancholy, long, withdrawing roar,
Retreating to the breath
Of the night-wind, down the vast edges drear
And naked shingles of the world.

Matthew Arnold, "Dover Beach"

In this perhaps his best-known poem, Arnold saw clearly the state of faith in his own mid-Victorian England, and inadvertently but accurately foresaw Western nations for much of the twentieth century. During the early part of the century, while institutional Christianity was strong and still had a considerable influence on society, there was some evidence of a weakening of spiritual life within the churches. At the end of the twentieth century, evidence of its frailty was conspicuous. Considered unworthy of serious consideration by our media, banished from our public schools, and viewed as quaint by our cultural gatekeepers, "the sea of faith," in social and political terms, is a small pool at best as we lurch past the starting gate of this millennium.

Christianity dwindled for a number of reasons. Secularization—an ideology as well as a process—trivialized transcendent matters, while certain forms of Christianity were susceptible to secularism and at times scarcely distinguishable from the surrounding culture. Sectarianism, fostered by fear of the secular world view, caused people of faith to withdraw from cultural engagement; in the process, intentionally or not, many became supporters of an almost mindless status quo. Christians between these poles felt discouraged and uncertain. Even though faith as a decisive factor in everyday life became cloistered in the private fortresses of church and home, surprising to most, a new wave of interest in matters spiritual began washing over North America.

Some, of course, wonder if this resurgence of faith was driven by the various agendas of American life, and particularly by the rise of the "Religious Right," politically and religiously conservative Americans who, out of angst over the moral drift of their nation, want to bring about change. Given the worldwide cultural and political influence of America, what they do has a ripple effect across national boundaries.

This book's purpose is to help Christians around the world steer clear of the secular/sectarian polarization and, at the same time, avoid the paralysis of taking a middle road. To move into a new way of thinking, I've had to re-evaluate the assumptions of my own church heritage, which tended to view the world as either unimportant or unredeemable. Since taking part in public debate, be it at the seat of our federal government, in a Supreme Court intervention, or on radio or television, I've learned to practice a language of public discourse in order to relate Christ's message to our social realities.

This book explores the evolution of that language framed between two biblical events: Babel and Pentecost. The story of Babel speaks of confusion, of a society misunderstanding its role in creation: this is my place of departure. The Hebrew day of Pentecost is a fitting image of the Christian life: the barrier of different languages removed, people were able to hear the gospel in their own languages, and thereby to achieve a common understanding of the task ahead.

This book is divided into seven chapters. Chapter 1 examines the reasons for our loss of a Christian witness within the public square. Chapter 2 digs into the Old Testament to learn what the Hebrews, as people of faith, believed a nation should be. Chapter 3 moves on to the New Testament to reveal Christ's call to his kingdom, and ends in Chapter 4 with an examination of what it really means to "think Christianly." Chapter 5 poses what we can learn from the history of Christians and Rome. Chapter 6 investigates pluralism and asks the question, "Is it just a modern Babel?" Chapter 7 ends with learning to speak a new language of faith and instilling passion into one's nation.

The genesis of this book began when I saw our son, Murray, as he received his undergraduate degree from Trinity Western University. As he walked across the stage I wondered what I could put into his hands that would help him (and his generation) understand the call of Jesus Christ today. This, then, is my offering to Murray, our daughter Muriel, and their respective spouses, Catherine and Jesse, and our grandchildren, Pearson, Olivia and Brycen. It is my attempt to understand the simple and yet complex message and life of our Lord to this world, in this age.

WITH THANKS

There are many who have greatly helped me in this process: Kathryn Dean, who in the early stages helped me with the primary structure and assumptions; Darrel Reid and Bruce Guenther, who did considerable research and writing and assisted me in many ways to think through our religious past, as well as Debbie Fieguth, who helped in research; Audrey Dorsch, who gave special assistance at a critical point in the writing; and those who carefully read the manuscript at various stages and offered pointed recommendations: Bruce Clemenger, Aileen Van Ginkel, John Kessler, Richard Mitchner, Paul Marshall, Don Posterski, John Redekop, Ian Rennie, Gerald Vandezande, and John Vissers. A special thanks to Susan Travis and Ruth Whitt for their loving assistance in helping with the manuscript. And finally to Larry Willard for his enthusiasm in this project.

In the end, what is written here, its style and perspectives, are mine. I do hope this material will provoke further research and writing, so that as Christians we will better understand our times and, in that understanding, know better the strategies to take (1 Chron. 12:32).

1

Why Twentieth-Century Christians Withdrew from Political Life

The United States has clearly drawn a line between church and state, yet familiar to their political speeches is the classic ending, "and may God bless America." Jingling in American pockets and purses is the coin reminding its users that "In God we trust." The driving force of a secular agenda has not been able to wipe out this refrain of believing and trusting in God.

As I walk up to the Peace Tower on Parliament Hill in Ottawa, I'm filled with a sense of history, destiny and goodwill. At our inception as a nation in 1867, the Fathers of Confederation chose "Dominion" from Psalm 72:8 (KJV): "He shall have dominion also from sea to sea, and from the river unto the ends of the earth." Growing up in this country, it seemed to me that a biblical vision shaped our very soul.

But there is a cultural embarrassment over one's national spiritual heritage. The only time, it seems, that Christian faith is called on to serve is for ceremony or the funeral of a Canadian political or cultural icon.

✝

The changing views of Christians about politics never cease to amaze me. For much of the twentieth century, evangelical Protestant Christians in many countries stayed away from any kind of involvement in managing or running their country. At the heart of this response has been the view that since Jesus had little to say about how Rome should manage Israel or Judah, then Christians today should leave it alone, too.

That is changing.

I have lived in a country which for years the United Nations has awarded the distinction of being the most favored country in the world to live. This notation from the UN surprises me, for many of my fellow citizens look to warmer climates for their holidays and, compared to Americans, we don't seem to be very patriotic. Even though this is a nation greatly blessed with enormous resources and a democratic political system, there is deep sorrow among many Christians over the shattering influence that radical secularism and humanism are having on our nation. Concern is now being voiced over the loss of Christian values and the taking hold of a more radical vision, hostile to the biblical assumptions, which in our history has influenced our people and society.

In my travels I hear colleagues asking questions of what biblical faith means to them in their country. Years after the Tiananmen Square massacre in Beijing, a Chinese Christian wondered how the gospel could act as salt and light in his restricted world. I walked in the West Bank with a Christian Palestinian who agonized over Christians who, when traveling to Israel to see the holy sites, passed by the homes of Christians bulldozed by the Israeli government. In anguish he wondered, *am I to be silent because Western Christians believe that the existence of the State of Israel supersedes a biblical sense of justice?*

As well, we live with uncertainty. There is an explosive build-up of interest in ideas that are often increasingly more spiritual in nature. This is not just an issue for Christians who believe that history is

God's concern. Those of New Age varieties and of the many faiths that dot our hemispheres are caught up in believing that something mystical, cosmological and metaphysical is occurring. For Christians looking for formulas predicting the return of Christ, both the founding of the State of Israel and the millennial interest combine into making the study of Christ's kingdom more important than at other more recent times.

The question with which we struggle is, to what degree does Jesus care about what is going on in one's country, whether the United States, Thailand or South Africa? That is at the heart of our search as we look not just to the phenomenon of prophetic interest but to who we are in Christ and what the Scriptures have to say to us about our role in this, God's creation.

None of us comes to this question in a vacuum. We all come out of a tradition or heritage that shapes the way we think. Each of us reacts and responds to ideas and societal issues in particular ways. Three friends come to mind. Caesar Molibatsi in Soweto, South Africa, especially during the years of white rule, not only struggled with the heartache of passport restrictions and racism, but the nature of the witness of the gospel to both his community in Soweto and the ruling white minority. Ajith Fernando, writer, teacher and evangelist, ministers in a multireligious environment of Sri Lanka where Buddhism rules, all the while working on a strategy to bring peace to a nation wracked by war. Ramez Attalla in Egypt works to build unity among Christians during times of fundamentalist Islamic violence.

Like Caesar, Ajith and Ramez, Christians around the world engage in public issues, refusing to back into ghettos of fear or irrelevance, choosing rather to move into the public forum with a deep conviction that Christ calls us to be his people of faith in the public squares of our world.

THE SPIRIT OF BABEL

In early biblical history, people living in what is now Iraq built a city with a tower "that reaches to the heavens" (Gen. 11:4). On the surface, the project may have appeared to be a noble one—something of a large-scale urban renewal project providing people with homes and places of work. The plan to build the tower sprang from less than dignified motives, however; all they wanted to do was "make a name for ourselves" (Gen. 11:4).

Seeing that their objective was to make themselves as God, the writer notes God's response: "If as one people speaking the same language they have begun to do this, then nothing they plan to do will be impossible for them" (Gen. 11:6).

God confused their speech, scattering them all over the world:

> Come, let us go down and confuse their language so they will not understand each other. So the Lord scattered them from there over all the earth, and they stopped building the city (Gen. 11:7–8).

And fragmentation began.

> That is why it was called Babel—because there the Lord confused the language of the whole world. From there the Lord scattered them over the face of the whole earth (Gen. 11:9).

At Babel, in contravening God's command "to be fruitful and multiply and populate the earth . . . and multiply in it" (Gen. 9:7), humans chose the opposite—to remain together and accumulate power.

By confusing their language, they were divided. For what purpose? To prevent the cumulative power of consensual evil. The concentration within one group would, by centripetal force (that is, by driving and focusing toward the centre), intensify evil so as to cause the community to self-destruct.

The confusion of language did the opposite. It effected a centrifugal force that drove people away from the centre, thus breaking up the convergence of evil. By so doing, human existence was preserved. Confusion saved them. Later, at Pentecost, God again used diverse languages, this time to create an occasion of unity.

Babel is a fitting place of departure for the search for a way to speak about what living in a nation means to a Christian. The growing debate over what we should be in a world that rejects biblical norms and faith calls one to think about the language that speaks of what we believe is God's call to service.

HOW TWENTIETH-CENTURY IDEAS CHANGED THE LANDSCAPE

Revolutionary ideas spawned during the nineteenth century slowly gained momentum in the early twentieth century and profoundly changed the way people viewed the world. To understand the shifting of evangelicals away from engagement in public life, it is important that these major world ideas are understood as part of the backdrop against which evangelicals first turned away from their historical interest in shaping their world and then, toward the latter part of the twentieth century, took up the challenge again of being part of spiritual renewal in society.

1. Science and Religion

Charles Darwin's theory of evolution, published in *On the Origin of Species* (1859) and *The Descent of Man* (1871), sparked vicious debate and unheard-of controversy. The church experienced a kind of loss of innocence. At first the impact was gradual. Initially Protestant clergy saw it not so much as a threat to faith as an opportunity to widen the influence of the church. But in the end Darwin's theories were assumptions far more influential than just a theory about human origins.

Darwin tried to show that all living things had emerged from a single, primitive form of life over a long period of time involving an unthinking physical process—meaning God was not in control. His evolutional model posited change as resulting not from the intent of the Creator, but from random natural selection. The attendant notion of "survival of the fittest" saw the process of creation as ongoing and concluded that millions of beings are born only to die, for no other apparent purpose than for survival of the species. Darwin's ideas held that instead of creation existing for human benefit, natural law operates without regard for human values.

The Darwinian debate was not only a conflict between science and religion; in fact, many scientists argued that evidence from geology and biology disputed Darwin's theories. Rather it was a debate between those who wanted belief in God accounted for within scientific explanations and those who argued that faith has no place within discussion of the origin of creation. William Dawson, a Presbyterian churchman, warned the church of coming implications, saying that God's role as a governor of its inhabitants would be displaced. He saw that to remove God from science would result in a weakened faith in Christ. How right he was.

Underlying the debate was a growing belief in scientific methods. Operating with a rationalistic and materialistic approach in the search for knowledge, science tended to exclude belief in the supernatural and ridicule the miraculous. In the early 1800s, church leaders believed that obtaining knowledge about the world was a good way to learn more about the Creator and his creation. But by the end of the nineteenth century, this view had experienced a reversal: Christian faith no longer shaped science. Religion, although interesting and even helpful, was seen as being neither true nor essential in the search for truth. In fact, religion was viewed increasingly as standing in opposition to reason. The seed planted 100 years earlier was now in full bloom. As philosopher David Hume wrote, "Religion has lost all specificity and authority; it is no more than a dim, meaningless and unwelcome shadow on the face of reason." [1]

As the twentieth century dawned, few mainline Protestants resisted Darwinian ideas. Though their leaders considered Darwin's theories troubling, they did not see them as destructive. Instead, they tried to harmonize their faith with this new and respectable science. To this end, they sought to minimize Darwin's view that evolution explained the origin of humanity and emphasized that evolution described how God improved the creation. This accommodation reassured church members that the theory gave greater strength to the Bible.

Church leaders assumed an affinity between the Bible and science. To oppose this seemingly irrefutable scientific "fact" was, in their view, to be out of step with a rational and reasonable faith. Universities, many with roots in nineteenth-century evangelical

Protestantism, seemed to have little interest in jettisoning Christian faith. Instead, there was a growing conviction that in light of new thought and discoveries, a reappraisal of faith and fundamental assumptions was needed. This need to harmonize modern science and faith left mainline Protestant churches vulnerable to an even greater intellectual force that threatened to further secularize them from within.

2. Higher Criticism of the Bible

Of all the ideas of the 1800s that influenced Protestant churches in the Western world, the most significant—even more so than Darwinism—was the loss of confidence in the Scriptures as God's Word. At the heart of this shift was a critical study of the literary methods and sources used by the authors of the Old and New Testaments. By using modern or "scientific" methods of historical, textual, and literary analysis, this approach to the Bible generated skepticism about whether or not the Scriptures were trustworthy or authentic. The life and teachings of Jesus were challenged, and seminary professors and ministers ended up excluding portions of the Bible deemed not to be authoritative or believable. This means of studying the Scriptures led many of the mainline churches to adopt a theology that, in turn, radically reshaped them.

Although church leaders at first worked out an accommodation with these intellectual trends, the acceptance of the underlying assumptions of modern biblical criticism eventually eroded confidence in the Bible. Though this approach inspired some new methods of study and uncovered some important insights, such as a better understanding of the historical context and the personality and style of biblical writers, it inevitably led to the conclusion that the Bible is not a divine revelation but, instead, is a product of its culture, just like any other book of history or literature.

Historians saw this form of biblical criticism as a way for theologians and ministers to explain away morally repugnant stories and doctrines, such as God's commands to wipe out entire communities or the story of Jonah. Jesus also could be reinterpreted. Instead of viewing him through such doctrines as the atonement and resurrection, attention focused on his moral example and social teachings. Sin could be seen no longer as a radical break between God and humanity, but merely as a matter of ignorance that could be corrected by education. This shift away from an evangelical doctrine in part helped drive the process of secularization of the Christian church.

This loss of biblical credibility left mainline Christian denominations vulnerable to the full impact of liberal theology during the twentieth century and eventually would result in an internal spiritual bankruptcy and the loss of moral leadership in the church.

Though many church leaders did not accept the destructive conclusions of modern biblical criticism, its influence gradually robbed the Scriptures of their preaching power. Sermons concerned with the most recent biblical theories or social commentaries created an impression that the Bible is difficult and inaccessible.

3. Human Progress

Scientific methods not only gave credibility to evolutionary theories and biblical criticism, but also fit with the Victorian optimism about "progress." Science was evidence that with this "natural" ability to reason, along with a greater understanding of the universe, the human condition would get better. The material, social, moral, and spiritual advance of humanity appeared inevitable.

Optimism converged with post-millennial notions that the kingdom of God would be established after a long period of progress. Many were convinced that material, moral, and spiritual improvements would result from the enlightenment of human thought and action, heralding the installation of Christ's kingdom on earth. It seemed that the human race—at least in the Western world—was on the verge of being in full control of its destiny. Reminders of sin and evil were masked by what was viewed as the improvement of humanity. For example, the transportation system of roads, railways, and canals was constantly expanding. Newspapers, the telegraph, and eventually the telephone facilitated rapid communication. Mechanization found new ways to ease tedious and back-breaking tasks.

Industrialization provided the means for people to escape unproductive farms, shifting demographics almost overnight.

As the twentieth century came and went, it became obvious that the world was not on the edge of enlightened rule. While holocausts and war undermined human optimism, there was such an overriding trust in human potential that faith in God—as a means of explaining life—was shunted aside.

4. Christianity as Just Another Religion

The study of Christianity as just one religion, nothing more than one of many, helped to undermine still further the belief in the uniqueness of Jesus Christ. Protestants historically held a firm view of foreign missions as the ultimate act of dedication. But as early twentieth-century missionaries reported on the work of Christ in saving people from other religions, they did so to a growing number of parishioners who were being pressed by their ministers to question whether the Bible is true, whether Christ is divine, and whether he is the only means of salvation. Not only did interest in missionary enterprise drop off, the missionary focus turned to a concern for moral and social reform.

In this context, the view of Christianity as unique and distinct from other religions diminished, replaced by religious relativism, which saw Christianity as one of many faiths, one more product of Western civilization. Conversion to Christ was no longer considered a necessary part of the missionary message. Not surprisingly, enthusiasm for missions declined among groups influenced by a liberal theology.

5. The Social Gospel Movement

"[I]t is the business of the Church to set up on earth the Kingdom of God as a social organization based on the Golden Rule of Christ," decreed the Board of Social Service and Evangelism of the Methodist Church in Canada 1914.[2]

As the new century rolled on, the Western world began feeling the full impact of unrestrained capitalism. Gross inequities in income, poverty created by high levels of unemployment, erratic cycles of economic depression, rapid urbanization, the unpredictable religious make-up of massive numbers of foreign immigrants, and eventually the drought on the North American prairies during the 1930s gave impetus to a movement to address social ills and pushed church leaders to think about what the gospel has to say about the way these societal forces affect people.

By the end of the century it became obvious that this approach to the marketplace was inadequate. The principle of good works gave some relief, but it did not address underlying causes. In a sense, mainline Christians determined to bring about change were trapped: the underlying assumption of Darwin's theories was "survival of the fittest." If one agreed with that in natural history, did one not have to apply it to economic history? The growth of capitalism was given encouragement in this Darwinian context.

Some church leaders saw that human misery increased as capitalism took the upper hand. When education proved inadequate as a strategy for coping with changing conditions, the churches turned to government to set the moral standards.

By placing emphasis on achieving Christ's kingdom on earth, leaders replaced theological explanations for evil and suffering with secular explanations. Nineteenth-century ideas reinforced one another in laying the foundation of the Social Gospel Movement: an optimistic view of progress; the potential of humanity; the influence of Darwinism; and the radical reformation of biblical understanding by modern biblical criticism.

God as transcendent and intervening was replaced by God in nature and history. Distinctions between the supernatural and natural, church and world, were replaced with the secular. A social definition of Christ's kingdom replaced doctrines of sin, salvation, and redemption. Truth was more defined by its moral impact on individuals and society. Concern for this world overshadowed interest in the afterlife. Jesus' death was not seen as the sacrifice for the sins of the world, but rather as the expression of the supreme power of love. The "mission" of the church was reinterpreted to mean bringing home the kingdom of God, and by religious education and social reform.

In the beginning, their programs were quite modest; they called for conversion of industrial leaders, redistribution of wealth, and influencing society with Jesus' teachings. Theology reinterpreted Jesus' teachings to apply to an ethical program of social regeneration, with less emphasis on individual salvation.

The bloody events of the First World War were a wake-up call for the Social Gospel Movement. Its vision of progress was shattered. The Social Gospel's identification with the state robbed the church of its prophetic role by reducing God's activity to social reform and political activity, while minimizing personal conversion. In addition, Social Gospel theology was challenged by those who clung to a dispensational understanding of the kingdom. They believed the world was about to witness the physical return of Jesus Christ.

Leaders in the Social Gospel Movement considered their vision to be more than a response to changing social conditions. They believed that if their churches failed to find economic and social solutions, the church would lose the working classes to secular materialism. In its attempt to renew the church by making its message more "relevant," however, it ended up secularizing mainline Protestant churches from within.

6. Political Liberalism

At the end of the twentieth century, political liberalism was playing an enormous role in restricting religion to a private experience. Liberalism as a social and political theory does not mean being generous or broad-minded. Nor does it have anything to do with a particular political party. It is a life view that freedom and autonomy of the individual are of primary importance to society. Philosopher George Grant defines it as

> a set of beliefs which proceed from the central assumption that man's essence is his freedom and therefore that which chiefly concerns man in this life is to shape the world as we want it.[3]

Political theorist Paul Marshall notes three essential ingredients of liberalism: (1) the development of the independence of people and family though urbanization, a market economy and industrialization; (2) an attempt to build a nonreligious political system that would solve the problems created by religious wars; and (3) the growth of rationalist and enlightenment philosophies that encouraged antidogmatism and the belief in human progress through reason.

Liberalism stresses individuality, freedom, individual autonomy and rights, the separation of religion and politics, reason, tolerance and the nonimposition of belief. It asserts that a neutral political system provides a sanctuary of tolerance for many different views. In theory, its creed is that it has no creed: its objective is to provide a framework within which each person can pursue his or her own freely chosen life, in which each tolerates the other; each view is accorded equal respect, and no view is imposed upon another; and the state is neutral. Individual freedom is vital to the workings of a democratic state—it is an idea found in the ministry of Jesus and expressed throughout the Gospels, although always within the framework of putting the interests of others ahead of one's own.

But liberalism is not neutral toward conflicting theories of the human good. By promoting human autonomy as the ultimate good, it undermines distinctive and traditional communities and replaces them with a uniform regime of individual choices. In forming public policy, liberalism is forced to take sides. In that sense, it is not neutral. While the legitimacy of the government to rule rises from the vote of each elector, the government must rule on a broader basis than individual rights. For example, a ban on smoking in public places overrides the rights of the individual in order to serve the greater good. Regardless of their intended benefits, such bans are not neutral in their view of what constitutes that good.

As individual freedom is made the highest good and the human will is exalted, then that which is beyond the human will is made to appear irrelevant. Freedom as the highest good cannot live alongside any other good, for any other good—if it is genuinely universal—would limit its autonomy. This world view is being imposed upon societies, often through the dominating power of the state, through elected assemblies, parliaments, and courts. The underlying assumption is that individualism is to be imposed. But this ends up replacing a genuinely pluralistic society with an enforced homogeneous society.

Liberalism as an ideology affirms that ultimate reality is not God but the autonomy of each individual. As such, God is pushed out of the equation of life. If individual freedom is the highest good and the human will is exalted, then that which is beyond the human will is irrelevant. Freedom as the highest good cannot live alongside any other good, for any other good—if it is genuinely equal—would limit its autonomy.

This world view increasingly has shaped Western society, often through the powerful influence of the state. The underlying objective is to impose individualism upon all, replacing a genuinely pluralistic society with a homogeneous liberal utopia.

7. Secularization

Secularization of life is a powerful and absorbing current. As secularization takes hold, Christian values and a Christian world view slowly recede and churches come to play less and less of a role in public life. This is not to say that Christian institutions disappear, that people no longer believe in Jesus Christ or that people stop attending church. For example, even though North American societies are highly secularized, high levels of Christian faith still remain. In a secularized society the message of Christ can continue to personally change people and influence human social movements. But secularization pushes faith outside of public life, so that Christian faith no longer abides in the hearts of the people.

In summary, these seven major ideas, then, have not only redrawn the belief framework for many in the West but have served to discourage Christians from taking hold of social and political issues.

PERSONAL REFLECTIONS

I now turn to a brief overview of how many of evangelical Protestant faith have withdrawn from their historic position of shaping their surrounding public world. Within the North American experience, in a matter of a few decades, we have moved from being a country greatly shaped by biblical leadership and values to a nation highly secularized.

I was born during the Second World War. My father, a minister, was of Swedish stock. His parents had left their homeland in search of religious and economic freedom. Dominated by a religious and political system that harshly treated anyone who chose to express Christian faith outside of the state church system, they left Sweden and settled on the prairies.

The society my Swedish grandparents found was a pioneer community, at the very edge of twentieth-century growth and development. The acknowledgment of Christian faith was fundamental to their national and provincial governments. The church was central to their community, and the expectation that this country was founded on a biblical understanding of life was not questioned.

The Great Reversal

As the twentieth century dawned, an increasing number of evangelicals made an about-face on their view of the role of Christ and society. There was a major reversal from the 1800s when a Christian morality profoundly shaped life in North America. From a central role in leadership, evangelicals moved to the side.

Three factors encouraged this ghettoization.

First, the fundamentalist–modernist conflict during the early part of the twentieth century convinced many evangelicals to have nothing to do with any groups other than their own. The growing influence of a liberal theology and the Social Gospel convinced many evangelical Protestants (sometimes called "fundamentalists" or "conservative Protestants") that old-line Protestants were too uncritical of new ideas. Evangelicals emphasized personal sin and conversion and viewed Social Gospel ideas as a sellout to worldly thinking. Biblical inerrancy—that is, believing the Bible is absolutely without error in any respect—became a major preoccupation. Energy and finances poured into evangelistic efforts and missions. Social and political involvement were left for others to worry about.

Second, the influence of pre-millennialism (a belief that Jesus would return before God brings in the 1,000-year reign) painted a gloomy view of the world, teaching that social conditions would get worse and worse leading to the second coming of Christ. As a son of this early twentieth-century evangelical community, I was immersed in the view that because Christ was about to return, the only really important thing we could do was to live a life in preparation for his return and work to warn others about the coming Kingdom. The assumption was that since his return is imminent (meaning at any time), it is therefore immediate (now). And because it is, to care about what government does is just a diversion from the real mission of the church.

These ideas were popularized by prophetic Bible conferences and the *Scofield Bible* in which Bible teacher Charles Scofield published the King James version with his notes, often including those written by John Darby, who had developed the theory of Dispensationalism. Believing that those in Christ would be taken away from the earth—raptured—provided a biblical rationale for Christians to keep apart from the world and made evangelism and missions more important than social activism. In this paradigm, the winning of converts was seen as the most important of all activities.

Pre-millennialism not only served as a catalyst for aggressive evangelism and missions but became a means of confronting post-millennialism (a view that Christ would return after the 1,000-year reign) which old-line Protestants seemed to prefer. It challenged the thinking that the kingdom of God was closer because of the moral and spiritual improvements brought about by so-called "enlightened" ideas of social reform. The newer churches simply had to point to the atrocities of the early 1900s to show how barbaric humanity is in contrast to the vaunted notion of progress. Although pre-millennialism nurtured a distinct subculture, it did provide the church with an important alternative way of seeing God at work.

A third reason why evangelicals withdrew was because of socio-economic differences. Most were not well educated, preferring training offered at Bible institutes (which nurtured a suspicion of higher education—"if theological liberalism came from seminaries and universities, then best avoid them" was the logic) over education offered at universities. As well, many evangelical Protestant churches tended to attract fewer professionals than did mainline churches.

By the 1960s many evangelical groups were leaving cultural isolation behind. In addition, sheer numerical growth helped them become cumulatively the largest and most robust religious community in North America, and increasingly in Latin America, Asia and Africa. Despite being seen by the secular press as narrow-minded, unsophisticated, belligerent and rural-sectarians, evangelical groups created a vast interlocking network of institutions and organizations that included theological education, campus youth ministries, missionary work, publishing and broadcasting worldwide.

Why are Evangelical Christians now Interested?

In 1966 Billy Graham invited 1,000 church leaders to Berlin to ask them what they should do in evangelism. Out of that emerged the 1974 Lausanne Congress in which some 2,400 delegates met over the matter of reaching the world for Christ. Anglican pastor and author John Stott edited the *Lausanne Covenant,* which became the basic document of agreement calling on Protestant Christian believers everywhere to work cooperatively from a basis of biblical orthodoxy in worldwide evangelization.

Though the horrors of the First and Second World Wars, the Jewish Holocaust and the "killing fields" of Asia in the 1960s and '70s reminded us of human depravity, it seemed to be the moral dilemma of the abortion crisis in the 1980s that galvanized action among evangelical Protestants, Roman Catholics, and Orthodox believers. Governments chose to distance themselves from the moral and ethical debate. At the same time, many Christians saw the need to challenge and change governments to reflect a Christian ethic. As one pastor put it, "If government is going to influence society this much, then we had better influence government."

During the post-war period of the 1950s and '60s, many saw the role of government as the prime engineer of society. Under U.S. President Johnson's War on Poverty, and Canadian Prime Minister Trudeau's social vision, more and more government viewed itself as an instrument not only to protect its people but to manage society.

The concern became more acute when Christians realized a primary assumption of this increasingly proactive government was founded on a liberal understanding of creation and individual rights. This dominating liberalism viewed faith as good for individuals or congregations, but not as something to be brought into the values and modes of operation of public life. As the twentieth century moved along, Western governments operated within the framework that belief in God was okay for their people but in their public discourse, only humanity was at the centre. Any notion of God was to be held at arm's length.

With the explosion of Christian faith worldwide and the increasing reports of Christians in the United States taking a more active role in their own country's affairs, a growing body of writing developed, calling on followers of Christ to begin with the understanding that governments are a gift of God and Christ's followers are to be stewards of that gift, including personal participation in political life.

What do We Mean by 'Christian'?

To answer this question, we must first agree on what we mean when we talk about how Christians might influence their nation.

First, "Christian" can be used in a weak sense to mean a country with some connection to the Judaeo-Christian heritage. Though almost every country in the West, from the late Roman Empire until 1800, was "Christian," many political and social realities were as far from New Testament Christianity as you can get.

Second, "Christian" can also refer to a nation in which there are many individuals who claim to be Christian. However, having a lot of Christians does not guarantee that what a society does is Christian. For example, note the former racist policies of South Africa. Genuine

Christians can get caught up in policies that are anything but Christian. So in the end, the presence of Christians might paint a picture of a country that is religious but not necessarily Christian.

Third, the term "Christian" can refer to a society that reflects the ideals and principles of Scripture. In such a society, the people are not just talking about doing God's will, but are doing it. An American historian comments,

> Although we would not expect perfection, we would expect that a 'Christian' society in this sense would generally distinguish itself from most other societies in the commendability of both its ideals and practices. Family, churches, and state would on the whole be properly formed. Justice and charity would normally be shown toward minorities and toward the poor and other unfortunate people. The society would be predominately peaceful and law-abiding. Proper moral standards would generally prevail. Cultural activities such as learning, business, or the subduing of nature would be pursued basically in accord with God's will. In short, such a society would be a proper model to imitate.[4]

Making these three distinctions helps us avoid equating our own political ideals with what we learn in Scripture. Getting caught up in assuming they are the same leads to idolatry and an irresistible temptation to national self-righteousness. These definitions call us to be careful in using the term "Christian nation." It is a fuzzy term that can make it difficult for Christians to be active, especially if it produces a distorted and overinflated view of any one country as being distinctly or uniquely Christian.

Corporate and Individual Christianity

Two major ideas have guided Christians in acting on Christ's call to "be in the world but not of it." On one side, there is "corporate" Christianity—the Christendom model—and on the other side, "individual" Christianity.

Corporate Christianity's first expression occurred in the fourth century, when Emperor Constantine made it the state religion. Christianity changed over several centuries, from an obscure sect worshiping a Jewish rebel, to a major world religion that sought to apply Christ's teachings to the political structure of the world's then greatest power. For the next 1,200 years this approach was used and, even when the church was divided by the Reformation, this Christendom model was included in the Protestant church through the teachings of the early reformers: Luther in Germany, Zwingli in Zurich, and Calvin in Geneva.

At the heart of the Christendom model is the belief that God deals not only with individuals, but also with nations. Based on the dealings of God with the children of Israel, it sees beyond the salvation of individuals to the formation of a godly society. Salvation is viewed as more than an individual matter; it extends to include families, communities, and ultimately the state. This model holds that nations which, through their rulers, seek to obey God will be blessed in this life, and nations that disobey will be judged.

To accomplish the task of constructing a godly society, the church and civil magistrates worked out various kinds of alliances. Ideally this relationship was to be reciprocal: the rulers had responsibility for ensuring the economic strength of the church, for passing godly legislation, and for restraining evil within society so that the church's teaching would have its intended impact. The church, for its part, was responsible for pointing the way of salvation, instructing people in their duties toward God, and supporting those whom God had placed in authority over them. The result, then, was to be a society that was Christian in its beliefs and godly in its life.

Inwardly, the aim was to bring all its members to the knowledge and worship of God; outwardly, although not all its individual members would become good Christians, it was hoped that at least they would display godly character in the world.

Even with such worthy ideals, such a system needed power to ensure that people conformed. Despite the imperfections of the Christendom model, those who supported it believed that it was based on Scripture and that in the end it would ensure Christian patterns for living.

The opposing view to corporate Christianity is "individual" or "believer church" Christianity. In this model it is not assumed that people will be socialized into a church. Church affiliation is a matter of personal choice. While reformers were reworking the old corporate model, the Anabaptist movement of the sixteenth century was a major force in shaping Christianity. Menno Simons, best known for leading the Anabaptists (better known as Mennonites), emphasized that a person needs to be old enough to make a conscious choice to follow Jesus Christ (and thus to be baptized), which eliminates infant baptism as a means of salvation.

At its heart, individual Christianity sees the relationship of the individual to God as being the context in which the most important expressions of Christian experience take place. This relationship is to be sought through Scripture reading, prayer, and living a Christlike life.

Anabaptists accused Christendom of confusing works—which cannot earn salvation—with God's grace, and of not being serious in living the Christian life. This confusion, they argued, resulted in an emphasis on good citizenship that effectively lifted the requirements the gospel places upon individuals themselves. Anabaptists argued that society would never become Christian: society was at best made up of redeemed individuals.

These two views, though often in opposition, are never completely distinct. The aim of corporate Christianity is the regeneration of society. Individual Christianity does not reject the broader societal implications of the faith. Indeed, Anabaptist groups, who criticized the Reformed societies of sixteenth-century Europe, built in Russia, for example, alternative Christian communities. These two views usually have had a transforming effect upon each other.

Does the Bible Call Us to Engagement?

This is the pivotal question. Is there clear direction for Christians to take on the running of society? Given that the Bible is so foundational to all of Christian life, this issue strikes at the very centre of any discussion.

Over the past few years, the story of William Wilberforce has been often used to describe the balance of being a Christian who is in the world but not trapped by the ideas of the world.

Wilberforce was a young Member of Parliament in England at a time when the slave trade was considered to be one of the primary economic pillars of the British Commonwealth. Horrified that slavery had become an important pillar of the British economy, he joined with a group of associates, called the Clapham Sect, and set about to force the House of Commons in London to reverse its position on slave trade.

The effort was massive. It took him almost to his death. He lost friends and was misunderstood. But in the end, remaining faithful to the Christ he followed, finally at four o'clock on the morning of February 4, 1807, Members of Parliament in the House of Commons voted to abolish slavery in the Commonwealth.

After being ridiculed and defeated, finally after many years, Christians led by Wilberforce brought about a world change to one of the most violent and degrading human practices. It came about because thoughtful and committed Christians believed that Christ cares about justice and truth within the public realm of leadership.

CONCLUSION

There is a danger, for those living in a country with a strong Christian heritage, to sit back and let others lead. No reflection is so powerful as that of Martin Niemöller, pastor and church leader in Germany during the rise of the Third Reich. He wrote,

> First they arrested the Communists—but I was not a Communist, so I did nothing. Then they came for the Social Democrats—but I was not a Social Democrat, so I did nothing. Then they arrested the trade unionists—and I did nothing because I was not one. And then they came for the Jews and then the Catholics, but I was neither a Jew nor a Catholic, and I did nothing. At last they came and arrested me—and there was no one left to do anything about it.

What do the Scriptures have to say about our role within the public sphere, and how should our lives be lived out as followers of Jesus of Nazareth? I believe that when Jesus called us to occupy until his return, he didn't instruct us to build spiritual fallout shelters.

2

What the Old Testament Says about Nation Building

As we search for an understanding of what God might expect a nation to be, the first place to look is the Old Testament. There we see how a nation should be constructed under God's direct counsel and presence. Although we are to be careful not to overuse this historical and unique example, it offers us clues to what a nation under God might look like.

✝

The Old Testament is an obvious place to begin our search for a biblical model for a nation, but how should this material be treated? There are three ways to interpret Old Testament material to preserve its integrity.[1] These provide windows through which we can view the stories, promises, and histories of the Scriptures as emblematic of how God interacts with his people.

The first window shows us God at work among his people. At this level of interpretation, the stories are seen as historical, but the lessons (the key factor) emerge from the principles.

For example, God's call to Abraham to raise up a people to live in accordance with the covenant is a picture of God calling out a people. The principle here is that God calls people who will follow.

The second window offers a vision of the future, when life will be ruled by God. According to this level of interpretation, even though a text may refer to the present, it also may be speaking of the future. Zechariah's vision is an example. He writes that the Lord said to him,

> I will return to Zion and will dwell in Jerusalem. Then Jerusalem will be called the City of Truth, and the mountain of the Lord Almighty will be called the Holy Mountain (Zech. 8:3).

Zechariah is describing a contemporary event, but he is also writing of a future time when God will rule the nation absolutely.

The third window presents the New Testament church as the inheritor of God's workings with the Hebrews. Take, for example, the Year of Jubilee. This celebration was to be a time when debt would be forgiven. The people and their land were to be given breathing time to start again:

> There should be no poor among you, for in the land the Lord your God is giving you to possess as your inheritance, he will richly bless you (Deut. 15:4).

This idea was picked up by the early church, which incorporated into its fellowship the premise that "there were no needy persons among them" (Acts 4:34).

The Old Testament is the story of God and the chosen tribes. We are not meant to link it to today, holus-bolus, and imitate Israel. Instead, we are to see it as a growing, moving, unfolding drama of God and human life. In looking for nation-building principles, rather than templates, we avoid the trap of assuming that promises to Israel apply to, say, Canada, the United States, or Western Samoa. They do not.

But it is appropriate that we learn from Israel, called to be a light to the nations: "I will keep you and will make you to be a covenant for the people and a light for the Gentiles" (Isa. 42:6). Again: "I will also make you a light for the Gentiles, that you may bring my salvation to the ends of the earth" (49:6). Thus, Israel was an example to other nations, and it points us to vital lessons.

Israel provides us with a picture, a paradigm, a way of seeing a people in relation to their God. This pattern of God's will for a called-out people is surely of interest to us thousands of years later. It is helpful to read the "Maker's instructions" when attempting to construct a nation.

To get at the essentials of nation building, we can identify six periods in which God dramatically interacted with his people: creation; the fall; the Abrahamic covenant; the laws of Moses; the kingly reign of David; and the message of the prophets. These give us a framework to construct an understanding of God's relationship to his creation.

The study of creation helps us see political and social life on God's broad stage. The fall of Adam and Eve brings us face to face with our individual failings and failed relationships: having turned away from its Creator, society is broken and the creation is alienated. Abraham learns of God's covenant, on the basis of which a socio-political community can be sustained. The laws given to Moses lead us further into the covenant; now society has laws and ethical mandates that specify how people should live together. King David's reign provides a particular political setting in which this covenant is worked out in detail. The prophets' stinging rebukes and powerful ethical challenges provide a counterpoint to the building of an understanding of what God has in mind for his people as they live out their lives in the nations of this planet.

From the outset we are overwhelmed with the reality that the earth is the Lord's, owner of all. Everything is subordinate to God's ownership. Stewardship is a moral obligation from which we draw the four ethical principles that guide how we should live: shared resources, work, growth, and accountability.

The first principle is that resources are to be shared. The bounty of the earth is given to humans only in a trustee relationship. The Genesis story of creation disproves the view held by those who believe they have prior claim to land because their ancestors were among the first immigrants. All of creation is God's and is a gift. The created man and woman who inherit God's image are given the task of caring for creation. As legitimate as private land ownership is to Israel, it is subsumed under the overarching principle of the lands being of benefit to all.

The second principle is that work is a gift from God, instituted before the fall. "Be fruitful and increase in number; fill the earth and subdue it" (Gen. 1:28). God as a worker passes it on to human creation. "The Lord God took the man and put him in the Garden of Eden to work it and take care of it" (Gen. 2:15). As we are called to tend the environment, we are also called to work.

Third, growth is a result of our labour: "Be fruitful and increase" (Gen. 1:28). Growth is a principle inherent in creation. The cycles of plant life manifest the inner nature of creation—to grow and reproduce. But growth requires tending. A field left to itself will choke with weeds. A fruit tree left alone will produce scrawny fruit. At the heart of creation is the balance of growth and control. To cultivate the land or prune the tree is to aid creation. Within the earth there is sufficient food-growing ability to satisfy the needs of all. However, greed, the drive to produce more and more without regard for the shared-resources principle, abuses creation.

Fourth, while we are at the centre of creation, tending and overseeing, humankind is accountable, for we are linked to other elements of creation.

> Let us make man in our image, in our likeness, and let them
> rule over the fish of the sea and the birds of the air, over the

livestock, over all the earth, and over all the creatures that move along the ground (Gen. 1:26).

To understand Yahweh (a Hebrew word for God) is to recognize the integrity of creation: life forms are interconnected. Each part of creation has the right to its own existence. But human leadership has a moral obligation to set limits to ensure the rights of all. Hoarding or private ownership without regard for the rights and needs of others simply does not figure in the scene of creation. "Dominion" does not mean "domination." "What is mine is mine" does not fit with creation.

The creation account provides us with operating principles that enable us to construct a model for God's will as we live in our nation/state.

The Fall: The Impact of Human Sin

The devastation of sin broke the harmony of creation and humanity, pitting one against the other, and changed the relationship of God to creation. Living in that "fallen" world, we strain and peer through a clouded window as we struggle to make sense of our relationship to God.

Living on this side of that cataclysmic break, it is hard to grasp its vastness. The turning of the human will from the Creator was enabled by one of God's former leading angels, Lucifer. (One-third of the angels had followed Lucifer, who was senior along with Michael and Gabriel, who led an attack against God and encouraged both the woman and the man to disobey Yahweh.)[2] Human beings entered a different phase when they disobeyed, losing their purity and intimacy with the divine.

Then the eyes of both were opened, and they realized they were naked; so they sewed fig leaves together and made coverings for themselves (Gen. 3:7).

What was natural became an embarrassment. They not only hid from each other behind the covering of leaves, but tried to hide from

God in the trees. The resulting impact was global. The relationship between Creator and created disjoined, and the man and the woman were set at odds with creation.

The fall violated the principles established under creation. The principle of shared resources was turned upside down. Resources became the object of greed and envy. The powerful hoarded rather than shared. Instead of care for the environment, abuse and pollution became the accepted standards. God's human creation became a means of oppression and of subjection.

Within this paradigm of failure and fallenness, the call to work is not abrogated. Indeed, it is affirmed. God, while forcing human creation out of the Garden of Eden, made an accompanying stipulation: "By the sweat of your brow you will eat your food" (Gen. 3:19). Whereas the responsibility of work was predicated before the fall on the idea that caring for God's world was a joy, after the fall it became an obligation. Along with this requirement came a promise. God always gives creation a means of going on. Implicit in the call to eat by the sweat of one's brow is the promise that there will be opportunity to work. Thus, there are now two work-related principles: work is an obligation, not only a joy; but, further, work is assured. Corrupted, however, work, like the creation, is distorted, abused,

> a commodity to be bought and sold, with little care or responsibility for the working human being. Work becomes a slave of greed, a tool of oppression, a means of replacing God with one's own ambition, even an idol in itself for some.[3]

The principle of healthy economic growth in which the creation is served is violated; creation is used rather than being served. That which was created for the good of others becomes that which is worshiped. This worshiping of growth loads an unbearable burden on those called to do the carrying. That which was seen by the Creator as a gift becomes the goal.

Economics then becomes the measuring stick of success instead of an expression of blessing. The principle of using resources for the good of all is turned into a tool of greed. The too-late-wise Solomon reflected on this unquenchable thirst for more:

Whoever loves money never has enough money; whoever loves wealth is never satisfied with his income. This, too, is meaningless. As goods increase, so do those who consume them. And what benefit are they to the owner except to feast his eyes on them? (Eccl. 5:10f.; cf. 5:13f.; 6:1f.).

Hosea, the prophet, points out the damage of violating creation:

Because of this the land mourns, and all who live in it waste away; the beasts of the field and the birds of the air and the fish of the sea are no more (Hos. 4:3).

Worship drifts away from Yahweh to the gods of the earth. This shift tends to be discounted in our technologically sophisticated world, dismissed as archaic or melodramatic. Nevertheless, we ignore this power struggle at our own peril. We fumble in our attempt to find God's rules for nation building if we ignore these obvious signs of our fallen creation.

Yahweh's demands to defend those who are trapped by the power brokers of economic domination run at cross-purposes to greed and self-interest. To follow in obedience to this God was as inconvenient then as today. There are clearly opposing sides. God's call is that creation is to enhance all. Fallen human impulses are reduced to self-serving concerns.

The building of a nation requires one to be realistic about human nature. Romanticizing our nature leads to seeing human failing not so much as the result of individual fallenness as having a societal cause. To ignore the nature of individual sin is to discount the obvious: "The heart is deceitful above all things and beyond cure" (Jer. 17:9). This is a good reminder for nation builders. Philosopher Immanuel Kant wrote, "From such warped wood as man is made, nothing straight can be fashioned."

The story of God and the Hebrew tribes culminates at the time of Noah, when punishment almost ended the human race. God saved Noah's family, and from this small family another civilization grows. It, too, however, runs into trouble, ending with the confusion of language at Babel. Meaning "the on-earth entrance into the heavenly or

celestial," Babel was built for the god Marduk.[4] The word has come
to mean the confusion of tongues, or "babbling."

In violation of God's call to populate the earth, humanity con-
centrated in one location; only one language was spoken. To break up
the human race into different linguistic groups was to minimize the
power of colossal evil of one large, unified group. God's intention in
doing so was to preserve humanity. In the story, as Wright comments,

> one can see the mercy and grace of God which uses that very
> effect of sin as a dike to save the human race from being totally
> engulfed in the self-destruction of unified evil.[5]

Because of Babel and the resulting confusion, civilization can
continue.

The Covenant: A Redemptive Move in Forming a Nation

The Genesis record then turns to a plan and solution. It would
take centuries to fulfill, but it would address the plaguing problem of
human sin. The story now revolves around Abraham and Yahweh's
covenant, and leads us to understand God's intentions for the people
of the covenant.

Out of its simple beginnings, this ragtag assortment of Semitic
tribes became a nation of substance and importance. It was not some
mythical or prehistoric world. It was a world of various languages,
nations, peoples, and ways of thinking.

Yahweh's choice of the Hebrew people was not a matter of selecting
from among many groups. It was, instead, the making of a new people.
Beginning with one family, God started a new tribal entity. Abraham's
homeland was Ur, in Babylonia, a sophisticated and culturally advanced
community. With outstanding architecture and complicated religions,
Ur was famous for its economics and political influence.

Leaving home, Abraham began his wanderings with a promise:
"Leave your country, your people and your father's household and go
to the land I will show you" (Gen. 12:1).

The building of a new people called for a special progenitor. God
saw in Abraham a person who would listen and trust. This was

remarkable, for the people of Ur worshiped a number of gods. From a civilization of many gods, Abraham made an abrupt turn to a belief in one God.

Then came the Word:

> I will make you a great nation and I will bless you; I will make your name great and you will be a blessing. And I will bless those who bless you, and whoever curses you I will curse; and all peoples on earth will be blessed through you (Gen. 12:2–3).

This was the covenant, the promise. On the strength of this, Abraham proceeded. We watch as the idea of covenant becomes reality.

Nation building is tough. It calls for people with determination, vision, and competence. For a country in its early stages, or when renewal is needed, risk-taking leadership is vital. Movements inevitably centre on visionaries. It took an audacious Abraham to move his people across unknown and dangerous territory on the basis of a promise from an unseen God. Two principles are at work here: (1) a nation will flounder without capable, vision-driven leaders; (2) Abraham operated with a deep conviction that the God to whom he spoke was real and could be trusted. Vision, in a national sense, is more than a dream for mining the potential of a nation; it sees the nation within the global community.

The word "covenant," as it is used here, means an agreement between two parties in which there is both a promise and a responsibility for each to fulfill his or her side of the agreement.

At its heart, it is a conversation. God called and Abraham heard. He raised objections with God about the promise of a vast progeny. It seemed hollow, as Abraham as yet had no children and, given that he was already an old man, the likelihood of his having children was slim (Gen. 15:2; 17:17). When promised a land, Abraham wanted to know how he would recognize it (Gen. 15:8). Lot, his nephew, was living in Sodom, a city God said would be destroyed. Abraham actually entered into negotiations with God, attempting to preserve the city (Gen. 18:23–33). Following God's instructions, he took Isaac, his only son born to Sarah, to the mountain for sacrifice (Gen. 22:1–14). Through the working-out of the covenant, God allowed Abraham to

ask questions, to press for greater consideration of Sodom, to be faithless in the promise of a son by Sarah, and to lie to a foreign king about
his attractive wife.

By promise of the covenant, God would make of them a "great
nation" (Gen. 12:2), great by virtue of its inherent goodness.
Goodness attracts. The law of sowing and reaping is at play here.
Israel would be great, measured not by power and military might, but
by a different standard.

There was another side to the covenant: Abraham had a duty to
perform, a promise to keep. First, to trust in this deity. "Abraham
believed the Lord, and He credited it to him as righteousness" (Gen.
15:6). It was out of this deep and all-encompassing belief that God
made the promise:

> On that day the Lord made a covenant with Abram and said,
> "To your descendants I give this land, from the river of Egypt
> to the great river, the Euphrates" (Gen. 15:18).

God made the promise, but also required a response of obedience:
"Walk before me, and be blameless" (Gen. 17:1). Out of this would
come the more immediate reality of the promise of a specific land.
But out on the far horizon was the promise that "in you all the families of the earth will be blessed" (Gen. 12:3).

Part of the story of the spectacular rise of Abraham is tragic,
showing the damage unbelief brings. Abraham was doubtful about
his and Sarah's ability, in their old age, to have a child. Sarah sug-
gested that he impregnate one of her maids, Hagar, to ensure a child.
But Hagar's pregnancy infuriated Sarah. Abraham gave in to Sarah's
anger, and Hagar was driven into the wilderness with her young son.
Even with Abraham's weakness and the lack of faith he showed in
substituting something for God's promise, the plan moved ahead.
But a woman was badly treated and another people (the Arabs) was
raised up, eventually ending up in conflict with the children of
Abraham and Sarah.[6] This is a classic story of human interference in
God's agenda.

To Christians, this history is very important. It describes the making of a covenant between the Creator and the created. Abraham is

dignified: he is able to question God, negotiate, and fail, and still God is faithful. Thus, the cosmos, the Creator, and the created are integrally related.

MOSES, MT. SINAI, AND THE DECALOGUE

The exodus of the Jews from Egypt was extraordinary. It was an act of liberation for the descendants of Abraham, who for 400 years had labored, at times as slaves, in Egypt. During that time, the memory of God's promise to their father, Abraham, was kept alive. They retained their identity, even under the cruel hand of their taskmasters. But it was in the exodus that they became a nation, albeit without a land or constitution. Against the backdrop of being delivered from Egypt and spending forty years wandering the wilderness in search of the promised land, they received specific laws for living.

Now that they were on their own, not ruled by the laws and rulers of Egypt, they needed guidelines, those understood requisites a society needs to survive. This undertaking, as was Abraham's, was a covenant, a promise from God. But it was not detached from God's actions. It followed the mighty act of God in the exodus. It was action and speech; God acts and speaks, and the two are linked. This bedrock to their national constitution was law, but at its heart was a covenant from God to his people:

> Now if you obey me fully and keep my covenant, then out of all nations you will be my treasured possession. Although the whole earth is mine, you shall be to me a kingdom of priests and a holy nation (Exod. 19:5, 6).

What an extraordinary promise. But it also called for sacrifice on the part of this priestly nation to live up to the requirements of its calling.

The law had two parts. First was the Ten Commandments, which in concise terms described the requirements. They were the broad, ethical conditions which set the groundwork for the nation. The second part laid out the specific details that covered everyday living.

The Decalogue

As Yahweh had made a covenant with Abraham as the father of
Israel, so one was made with Moses. In the Ten Commandments, or
Decalogue, Yahweh made commitments to Israel, and, in return, obligations were imposed. God clearly lists those things that are critical to
sustain a people living together. As basic as they were to Israel, those
laws are also viewed by modern societies as essential for a working
community. No code of any other society is so explicit, succinct, and
all-encompassing for societal living.

The details are many, yet the essence of the covenant is found in
ten specific and precise calls that form the basis for all Hebrew law.
These ten principles were intended to define the parameters within
which the people would find the fullness of life and develop a rich,
rewarding relationship with their God and Creator.

> Hear, O Israel, and be careful to obey so that it may go well
> with you and that you may increase greatly in a land flowing
> with milk and honey, just as the Lord, the God of your fathers,
> promised you (Deut. 6:3).

These commandments were not only a moral code, designed to
assist people in developing their ideas about life, but specific commands, related to how people actually lived. They were directives by
the God of the nation. Thus, to disobey a commandment was not just
to fly in the face of the nation, but to defy God. The breaking of a law
would not only threaten the stability of the nation, but impair the
covenant or agreement with God.

To the Jews, the giver of this covenant is more than a lawgiver.
He is the God of the exodus—the liberator, the one who freed them
from slavery and bondage. The order is important. The one who res-
cues sets up the code for living. Liberation is always on the lips of the
giver of the law. Although the commands are prohibitive in nature,
at their heart is the principle of love: "Love the Lord your God with
all your heart, and with all your soul, and with all your strength"
(Deut. 6:5).

THE LAND

A people cannot live without land. For the Hebrew tribes, the conquering of Canaan was seen as God's fulfilling the promise. Today, as then, in the Middle East the essential point of conflict is land. Nothing triggers passion more than dispute over land. The Old Testament notion of land promised to Abraham, renewed in promise to Moses, and finally received by Joshua, was that it was given to them. This special promise was based on their understanding that the land they had received was bestowed by God; they could not take credit for having acquired it for themselves.

The principle at work here, apart from the specific promise to Abraham, is their vision that land was indeed a gift from God. People, be they wandering Semitic tribes or a modern, technological society, possess their land by way of a gift:

It is not because of your righteousness or your integrity that you are going in to take possession of their land; but on account of the wickedness of these nations, the Lord your God will drive them out before you, to accomplish what he swore to your fathers (Deut. 9:5).

Understanding that the land is God's gift kept the Jews from regarding it as their neighbours did. For the Jews, Yahweh was the reason for the land: the land came from God. This view was in contrast to the popular Baal notion of a god rising out of the land. Baal, the most prominent Canaanite deity, was believed to live in the netherworld. To raise Baal, and thus to ensure a fertile rainy season, Canaanites engaged in orgiastic worship, which included human sacrifice, sexual rites, and the use of "sacred" prostitutes. God strictly forbade such worship (Judg. 2:12-14; 3:7, 8). In sharp contrast, the Hebrew God was sovereign, above the land and nation.

THE DAVIDIC KINGDOM

Nation building was to reach its zenith under David, son of Jesse. The journey had been long and treacherous. By failure, trial and error, and direct instruction, the Israelites were learning about God's intention and rule over their lives. They were to be a different people, separate from their pagan neighbours, and, most of all, to live in constant remembrance of their allegiance and dependence. King David's rule is the most complete snapshot of what a nation under God is to be and do. It is here we see the sum of what the children of Israel had learned cemented into political reality. Looking back from our vantage point, we see how Abraham's vision and his covenant with God developed into the defined laws of Moses as the people left their nomadic existence for permanent settlement under their revered king.

The development of a state came slowly. In their early days, the Israelites were nomadic, living as a group of clans. Each clan had its own authority, but there was no class distinction. Central to the Hebrew nomads was the Ark of the Covenant, constructed by Moses after fleeing Egypt. It was carefully preserved, and there, once a year, the high priest made a sacrifice for the sins of the people.

During the times when judges ruled the twelve Hebrew tribes, from time to time a strong charismatic person would rise up and lead. But a judge had no government and operated with no central authority. He or she had no army or administration by which to rule. Only when Israel was threatened by an enemy would the people rally in support of the leadership and coordination role of the judge.

The pattern of development of the Hebrews was different from the city life of the people already in Canaan. In the beginning, as the Hebrews began possessing the land of Palestine, they developed farms rather than building cities. For 200 years after winning the promised land, they continued as a network of tribes, identified by their racial and religious heritage but without a single political or geographic home state.

The Hebrews acquired a king when Israel was confronted not just by the Bedouin raiders, but by the organized and disciplined armies of the Philistines from the north. When the famous and powerful judge Samson was killed, the Hebrews were thrown into chaos. After being pressured by the people, Samuel, the priest, anointed Saul as king. But there seemed little Saul could do to cobble together a strong army out of this tribal community.

That task was left to David, a young, brave and charismatic shepherd who replaced the terrible system of a frightened assembly of clans with what was the beginning of a nation. The people of Israel sang, "Saul has slain his thousands, and David his tens of thousands" (1 Sam. 18:7). David had no lineage to argue for a legitimacy to rule. His authority came from the people. They made him their hero. He raised a strong private army in his defence against King Saul, and then a standing army. He married Saul's daughter and, through an election of sorts (2 Sam. 5:1-4), was proclaimed king.

David took steps to create a united nation to defend the people against the Philistines, and he selected a site on which was built "the city of David" (2 Sam. 5:9). He eventually defeated surrounding states and ruled from the Gulf of Aqaba in the south to Syria in the north.

As David wrote his poetry and songs and ruled as king, his framework was God. To David, Yahweh was king, not only of Israel, its priests and leaders, but over all kings of the earth (Ps. 97:6). The entire construct of life, including earthly kingdoms (2:6-9) and the physical creation is under the rulership of God (47:3; 89:9-19; 93:1, 2). As ruler and Creator, the strategy for liberation and national rule falls within God's cosmic plan. All histories of all people are set within that plan, including those of Israel, Egypt, Assyria, and Babylon (48:4-6; 96:10-13).

David, as king of Israel, was regarded as the best example of what a king and ruler should be. Under his kingship, Israel reached her highest level as a civilization. David is remembered for honesty, humanity, and a deep regard for the creation. Today, Jerusalem, in his honour, is called the "City of David." Though King David's life was not spared from failure, his vision for his nation guided him in construction and management.

Psalm 72 is a reflection on the nature of nationhood and a prayer for Solomon, David's son, who will rule after his death. There are four cornerstones that structured this vision for Israel. From this we get a picture of the essential elements of what is required in a nation in which godly values reign.

A Nation Built on Justice and Righteousness

Justice and righteousness are used throughout the Old Testament as primary elements of godly rule. David prayed,

> Endow the king with your justice, O God, the royal son with your righteousness. He will judge your people in righteousness, your afflicted ones with justice (Ps. 72:1-2).

Justice refers to the activity of a lawgiver in carrying out the legal consequences of a verdict of law. *Righteousness* comes from a Hebrew root word which speaks of something "straight." It literally refers to accurate weights and measures used in everyday commerce. *Righteousness* means "rightness"; that is, what will measure up to the standard.

Under David's administration, the laws were to be clear for people to understand and were to be made public so that no one could claim he or she was unaware of them. They were to reflect what the nation, as a people, believed to be true. Only then does law become a standard against which behaviour can be measured. The standard will not vary from trial to trial; nor will it be interpreted to suit the self-interest of the judge. The rightness of the case will be judged with fairness.

A Nation Built on Effective Rule

In David's understanding, a nation was to provide its people with security and peace in which there was "rule from sea to sea" (Ps. 72:8). Citizens and outsiders would recognize it as a bona fide nation with political integrity, not one ready for the pickings of some exploitive raider. Within the country, the people could expect their rulers to lead and to contain violence: "He will rescue them from oppression and violence, for precious is their blood in his sight"(Ps. 72:14).

A Nation Built on Economic Well-Being

Regardless of the form of its economic activity, be it agricultural, technological, or world trade, a country needs a healthy economy.

The problem for all nations is that economics has become an idol. But that does not deny that for a nation to operate under God's mandate, economic well-being is God's will.

David's vision was of a prosperous nation: "Let grain abound throughout the land; on the tops of the hills may it sway. Let its fruit flourish like Lebanon" (Ps. 72:16). The basis of his economic vision is economic responsibility: "For he will deliver the needy who cry out, the afflicted who have no one to help" (Ps. 72:12). Economic blessings are linked to justice and righteousness, which by direct implication reminds us that economic well-being is not only for the few. A nation that does not fulfill the economic calling of God could hardly be called a "light to the nations."

A Nation Built on Caring for Those in Need

David places strong emphasis on caring for those in need: "He will defend the afflicted among the people and save the children of the needy" (Ps. 72:4). This theme is in line with God's constant reminder: those in charge are to be mindful of those who are in need, weakened, or unable to help themselves. Though this might sound like the social agenda of some political party, it is intrinsic to the theme and message of the Bible. Indeed, God evaluates nations on how they deal with the marginalized.

Psalm 82:3-4 reminds us,

> Defend the cause of the weak and fatherless; maintain the rights of the poor and oppressed. Rescue the weak and needy; deliver them from the hand of the wicked.

David is not advocating a particular socio-economic plan. The glaring tragedy is that under various systems, too often, defence of the poor and the sick is lacking.

David's leadership was built on a vision that God's rule over Israel required the nation to follow certain principles. His success in ruling demonstrates that his ideas were more than theoretical. From this we learn what is essential to godly rule, and from that we can extrapolate to our own national situation.

PROPHETIC RULE

After the rule of David, the nation was divided between Israel in the north and Judah in the south. This division served only to weaken the struggle to maintain national identity and governance against the onslaught of foreign nations. In a nation held for ransom, taken captive, and suffering its own political and social anarchy, prophets were called on to encourage, scold, and remind the people of God's will. It is to this group of people we turn to hear the clear word of God's call for nation building.

Israel as a nation had been called to break with ancient paganism. Central to their faith was their God, who controlled events in history. In this, worship of Yahweh contrasted sharply with surrounding pagan religions, which were polytheistic, with dozens of gods in pantheons. These gods, having no moral character, represented nature or parts of the cosmos. As well, they could be manipulated in rituals, as they were a re-enactment of myth. Thus, they could be made to bestow on the worshiper whatever he or she wanted. The gods made no moral interpretation of physical events.

Yahweh is different. All of life comes from God the Creator, and all events are under his control. Yahweh is not to be linked to nature, and therefore cannot be appeased by any ritual.

The high vision of the kingdom slipped downhill following David's rule. His son Solomon ruled in wealth and splendor, but increasingly became out of step with his father's vision. Nepotism, not calling or character, had decided that Solomon would follow. The privilege and wealth of the newly developed aristocracy divided the people into the powerful and the powerless. Solomon and the kings who followed him assumed that people were to be ruled and owned as subjects, an idea foreign to David. As well, the lavish lifestyles of the kings had to be paid for by someone. That meant taxes.

The kingdom eventually ran into serious trouble. With the division into Israel and Judea, it was not long before other nations raided and plundered both kingdoms. During this time, the role and presence of the prophets increased. They encouraged and chastised, always attempting to remind the people of God's faithfulness.

Prophets antagonized rulers as they proclaimed their visions of justice and righteousness. Their blazing pronouncements of God's rule and glory cut deeply into the mind-set of a people who too quickly slipped into the worship of other gods. It was the prophets' understanding of God's rule, however, that pulled them back to faithfulness. Their bold and rousing rhetoric stirred the people's hearts and fanned the flame of obedience. From their righteous anger came the words that foretold disaster and God's faithful care.

While the prophets served the Jewish nation, their soundings were inspired by more than immediate circumstance: their rhetoric was about an all-encompassing reign of God. That reign was not to be confined to Israel. The call of Jonah to go to a Gentile city is an explicit reminder that God's rule is not only Israel-centred.

THE RULE OF GOD

Running through the messages of the prophets are a number of themes that help us understand their vision of God's kingdom rule.

God's rule in Israel is redemptive. It has at its core a fourfold plan: politically, to free the Israelites from foreign tyranny; socially, to provide protection for family and community; economically, to free them from forced slavery and injustice; and, spiritually, to call them to remove themselves from foreign gods.

THE POLITICAL PLAN

Micah sees that in the last days,

the Lord's temple will be established as chief among the mountains. . . . Many nations will come and say, "Come let us go up to the mountain of the Lord, to the house of the God of Jacob." . . . The law will go out from Zion, the word of the Lord from Jerusalem. He will judge between many peoples and will settle disputes for strong nations far and wide. They will beat their swords into plowshares and their spears into pruning hooks. Nation will not take up sword against nation, nor will they train for war anymore (Mic. 4:1-3).

The themes of a kingdom ruled by God weave their way through this famous passage. Yahweh will rule over all and will teach us wisdom and truth. The downtrodden will receive justice, and war will be no more. Fear will be neutralized, and all nations will walk in his ways.

Isaiah looks forward to a Messianic age when, under a descendant of David, righteousness will rule and the people will be freed from oppression. There is no greater song of national unity and strength than that of the coming Messiah:

> And he shall be called Wonderful Counselor, Mighty God, Everlasting Father, Prince of Peace. Of the increase of his government and peace there will be no end. He will reign on David's throne and over his kingdom, establishing and upholding it with justice and righteousness from that time on and forever (Isa. 9:6-7).

The Social Plan

This God of Israel and Judah not only reigns over the earth, but protects the life of the people. Even in the difficult times,

> I will be with you; and when you pass through the rivers, they will not sweep over you. When you walk though the fire, you will not be burned; the flames will not set you ablaze. For I am the Lord your God, the Holy One of Israel, your Savior (Isa. 43:2-3).

The concern of the ruler is for the Israelites' welfare; they will be led again into the promised land. The words are reminiscent of the exodus from Egypt:

> I will bring your children from the east and gather you from the west. I will say to the north, "Give them up!" and to the south, "Do not hold them back." . . . Everyone who is called by my name, whom I created for my glory, whom I formed and made (Isa. 43:5-7).

They see the nation healed by God's presence, a time and place in which the king will bring unity. As a result, the nation will be "a light for the Gentiles" (Isa. 42:6) and will attract Gentile nations:

See, I have made him a witness to the peoples. Surely you will summon nations you know not, and nations that do not know you will hasten to you, because of the Lord your God, the Holy One of Israel, for he has endowed you with splendor (Isa. 55:4-5).

Central to social harmony is justice. Amos calls out,

For I know how many are your offenses and how great your sins. You oppress the righteous and take bribes and you deprive the poor of justice in the courts. . . . Seek good, not evil, that you may live. . . . Hate evil, love good; maintain justice in the courts (Amos 5:12-15).

The Economic Plan

Zechariah paints a vivid picture of the reign of God:

Before that time there were no wages for man or beast. . . . But now I will not deal with the remnant . . . as I did in the past. . . . The seed will grow well, the vine will yield its fruit, the ground will produce its crops, and the heavens will drop their dew (Zech. 8:10-12).

Along with the promise of economic well-being, there is a constant reminder of God's care and special love for people in need. Amos combines a promise and rebuke: to the poor, they will be remembered; to the powerful and wealthy, they are to understand their unfairness will be judged: "Hear this, you who trample the needy and do away with the poor of the land, saying, 'When will the new moon be over that we may sell grain, and the Sabbath be ended that we may market wheat?'... The Lord has sworn by the pride of Jacob: 'I will never forget anything they have done.'"

The Spiritual Plan

God's reign is political, social, and economic, but it does not end there. For the prophets, renewal is at the heart of Yahweh's rule. Even though the people are faithless, God will put laws in their minds and write them on their hearts (Jer. 31:31-33). To the people, God will continue to be faithful, even after long, hard years of struggle.

Jeremiah's resilient theme is that a time is coming when the kingdoms will be ruled by a righteous king:

> In those days and at that time I will make a righteous Branch sprout from David's line; he will do what is just and right in the land. In those days Judah will be saved and Jerusalem will live in safety. This is the name by which it will be called: The Lord Our Righteousness (Jer. 33:15, 16).

Amos' call was to bring the people back to faith and worship. The problem wasn't that they were not religious. Indeed, they were. The problem was that they were religious in the wrong way. Religious ritual was just not enough. Living right and being just were needed to give ritual any value:

> I hate, I despise your religious feasts; I cannot stand your assemblies. Even though you bring me burnt offerings and grain offerings, I will not accept them. Though you bring choice fellowship offerings, I will have no regard for them. Away with the noise of your songs! I will not listen to the music of your harps. But let justice roll on like a river, righteousness like a never-failing stream! (Amos 5:21-24).

The Universal Reign of God

Beyond the borders of Palestine, some prophets saw the reign of God as universal. Ezekiel describes this worldwide rule of God in the life of all humankind. He opens with a powerful statement:

> In the thirtieth year, in the fourth month on the fifth day, while I was among the exiles by the Kebar River, the heavens

were opened and I saw visions of God (Ezek. 1:1).

Ezekiel reminds us that at all times, in all places, "the Lord is there," a phrase on which he ends. Even though Ezekiel is a priest, he understands that God's domain is not limited to the sanctuary of the temple in Jerusalem but traverses the world, even to the exiled children in Babylon.

Daniel, while in Babylon, was called on to interpret the king's dreams, which had baffled the king's magicians and sorcerers. Ringing through Daniel's interpretations is the residual hope of God's kingdom, alive forever. Even though he was living in a pagan land, Daniel envisions this kingdom rule as applying not just to the Jewish world, but universally. Most prophets lived in Palestine; thus, their hopes were centred in that region, and with the Jewish people. However, since Daniel and Ezekiel lived in Babylon, they saw the future through a different lens. They envisioned a broader rule of God, extending beyond the borders of the promised land and including others besides the chosen people.

LESSONS FROM THE OLD TESTAMENT

The importance of reviewing some of the prophets is to hear their heart-cry for God's righteousness and justice in the way the nation is ruled. They defend the poor and widows. Their sharp cry cuts into the self-centred living of those with power and wealth. Living within a society steeped in the idolatry of the Mediterranean community, God's people are called to renounce their spiritual wanderings and return to worship the one true God.

There are three windows, so to speak, through which we can see God at work in the life of his people. We can interpret these scenes and apply them to how we live as disciples in our own country. Our first window on the Old Testament is the paradigmatic window, through which we look for the principles of the story; the second is the eschatological, through which we understand that the text is looking forward to God's full and final kingdom; and the third is the typological, through which we see the church inheriting the essential truths for its well-being. Thus we construct a vision of a nation.

Remember, we must not use the Old Testament to suggest what it does not mean. With that caution in mind, we see God's intention to raise a people and nation, which, in turn, serves us as we structure a nation today. A nation founded on those principles produces a healthy society reflecting the psalmist's belief that a nation is enhanced when the Lord's values reign: "Blessed is the nation whose God is the Lord" (Ps. 33:12).

The Old Testament helps us see God in four ways: concern for the creation, God's rule over all of life, God's covenants and promises, and God's expectation of obedience.

Out of this time/space cradle, the Messiah, Jesus of Nazareth, comes. The seeds of the Messiah's rule are evident in the rule of Yahweh in Palestine. We now move into the time of Christ's earthly ministry to see how the actual working of the kingdom moves beyond a nation and a particular people to a more integrated heart/mind reality.

Reflection on the Hebrew/Palestine experience is very important. Within this framework, we can work out a particular vision for a nation, applying what we learn, seeking to properly integrate that which God has shown in the Hebrew tribal model. From there, we proceed to the next stage to learn what Jesus of Nazareth had to say about being citizens and people of a nation.

3

Jesus and Politics

Did Jesus ever expect his followers to deal with Rome? If we wish to influence a country to adopt biblical values, is there any evidence that Christ called on us to express our concern? In a stressful socio-political environment rife with anger against Rome and intense expectations that the Messiah would rout their oppressors, Jesus had a surprising response to this cauldron of nationalism.

✝

My kingdom is not of this world. If it were, my servants would fight to prevent my arrest by the Jews. But now my kingdom is from another place (John 18:36).

Did Jesus intentionally preach a gospel that was to affect political theory or governmental management? Or, to put it another way, did the political ordering of a nation matter to Jesus and God's kingdom? I argue that Jesus was a political force in that day: his message struck deep at the existing ruling assumptions. However, Jesus was not announcing an alternative political theory. His message goes deeper into our self-serving interests; he speaks to all people, regardless of their political and social systems.

I also argue that Christ's gospel calls for Christian disciples to care for today's society, be it governments or major sectors of our public interest such as education, the media, the justice system, science, industry, and the arts. In Christ's kingdom, all of life is subsumed under God's creation.

British Anglican Church leader and scholar John Stott comments that Jesus' "whole ministry was political."[1] "Politics" refers to people as citizens living together in society. (The Greek word *polis* means "city," and *polites* means "citizen.") In speaking about Jesus and politics, I am not limiting my discussion to the science of government and the election of politicians or appointment of officials. Instead, through an understanding of Jesus and politics, we can see how we relate as citizens living in a particular country.

It is true that although Jesus did not participate in political ruling, he did influence and speak to those who had a role in governance. Nor did Christ form a political party or contest the rulership of Pilate or Caesar. But he did effect change. Jesus spoke a new message, upsetting the status quo by setting forth a challenge to old and self-serving assumptions and values, both those of the Romans and those of the ruling religious leaders.

First, as we examine Jesus' relationship to politics, we cannot apply faith to life until we are familiar with what Jesus intended his life, and the lives of the disciples, to accomplish. Second, the coming of Jesus cuts across the grain of our religious expectations by not being what we expect.

As noted in chapter two, running through Hebrew history is a belief that God would forever establish his rule. It was the hope of each Hebrew citizen to live to see this rule set in place during his or her lifetime. Even though hope was frustrated, a deep conviction remained that the Son of David would some day rule with justice and power.

THE SETTING

Because context means everything to the understanding of Jesus' words and ways, we need first to look at the social/political realities that cradled this advent.

Just prior to Jesus' coming, a revolt had been led by a Jewish family, the Maccabees. In 63 B.C. the Roman general Pompey annexed Palestine, bringing it under Rome's rule. Rome, while directly ruling Judea, gave much of its political oversight to the Sanhedrin, the Jerusalem city council. Thus, whatever Jesus said to the Jewish rulers implied commentary on Rome as well. In the north, the Jews were governed by a half-Jewish family, the Herodians. Divided up under different rulers and different forms of rulership, they were deeply embittered, their actions fueled by their deep desire for self-rule.

When Jesus arrived, the deep river of messianic hope was fed by two powerful currents, both wanting to secure national independence and stability. The Zealots, a Jewish party trumpeting a radical nationalism, were ready for war and were game to try to overthrow the Romans. Their deepening anger against the Romans was heightened by what they regarded as an unholy alliance between religious leaders and Rome.

The Pharisees represented a movement begun more than a century earlier, in part to protect Hebrew nationalism from the powerful cultural forces of the Greek (Hellenistic) forces. Rejecting the Zealots' agenda, they believed that God would send the Messiah only when the people strictly observed the law.

It is not surprising that Jesus' announcement of a kingdom met the people's expectations. Oppressed by foreign rulers and grieving over the treachery caused by the invaders, they rejoiced at Mary's (Jesus' mother's) words:

> He has performed mighty deeds with his arm; he has scattered those who are proud in their inmost thoughts. He has brought down rulers from their thrones but has lifted up the humble. He has filled the hungry with good things but has sent the rich away empty (Luke 1:51–53).

Even though it had been 600 years since they had returned from exile in Babylon, they still considered themselves in exile as long as they were under occupation by a foreign power. Jesus' kingdom announcement connected with their deepest aspirations.

THE COMING OF THE KING

Into history God came, and life would never be the same again. God had come to assert rule over all of life. Though we might regard the kingdom in terms of what it brings—salvation, justice, and healing—Jesus' coming is more radical. At the very centre of it is the right to rule, and power and authority to effect that rule.

By "kingdom" I mean that which is the rule and reign of the king: wherever the king is, that is the king's domain; whatever concerns the king, that, too, is the king's domain.

The kingdom's message was to save the sinner, not the righteous. The message presupposes that we are unable to correct our ways. "Blindness" is the appropriate metaphor. Not only can't we see, but we don't know we can't see. All human attempts to right our wrongs have failed and will continue to fail. God takes the task alone. Yahweh did not come because Israel was successful in creating a more just community or constructing a better political system, but because it could not. Simeon and Anna (Luke 2:25–38), who prayed for the coming of the Messiah, knew that the religious leaders, political insurgents, or pious faithful could not build this kingdom. It must be achieved by God's initiative. Even as the Earth is the Lord's, so was the need to take back what was rightfully God's.

But does Christ's kingdom also include political life? At first glance, Jesus gives the impression it does not extend to political concerns. However, a closer look shows that the opposite is true. What makes it unclear at first is that Jesus' analysis and prescription went deeper than what the people expected. Jesus not only followed Old Testament thought that God's rule included all aspects of life, but went further and announced a new provision—people could personally experience a rebirth.

This was not what was expected. The hometown folk in Nazareth were shocked at the description of the coming kingdom. When Jesus spoke of the less important members of society, those without power or influence, the townsfolk were scandalized. Jesus said,

> The Spirit of the Lord is upon me, because he has anointed me
> to preach good news to the poor. He has sent me to proclaim
> freedom for the prisoners and recovery of sight for the blind,
> to release the oppressed, to proclaim the year of the Lord's
> favor (Luke 4:18, 19).

They were not only surprised by what Jesus did, but also disappointed. Jesus did not pick up the sword to drive out the Romans, nor accept the public celebration on Palm Sunday and take possession of David's throne. The talk about power and authority concerned itself with the rule of one's own spirit. They were confused. There was no announcement of the overthrow of Rome. Jesus made it clear they should give to God what was God's. But what was God's? Everything (Rom. 11:36). And what was the meaning of the kingdom? Peter, frustrated by the apparent undoing of what the disciples believed was a new order, tried to defend Christ in the final hours before his death. Instead, the death pushed them into fear and despair.

Even the disciples, after three years of living with Jesus, asked, "Lord, are you at this time going to restore the kingdom to Israel?" (Acts 1:6). I suppose that if they thought Jesus' kingdom was going to throw out the Romans, it is not surprising that people today are confused by what Jesus had in mind about the relationship of the kingdom to a nation. They would not see the nature of the kingdom because they were looking for an immediate solution. It didn't occur to them that Christ's kingdom was to rule, first and foremost, over the heart.

Jesus radically changed their understanding of the kingdom. He redefined authority and power, and introduced symbols that were the opposite of what they expected. At the Last Supper, while the disciples talked about who would be greatest in the coming kingdom, Jesus picked up a towel and washed their feet. In a society layered with power, ritual, and rank—among both the Jewish religious community and the ruling Romans—taking on the role of servant was both dramatic and political, because it challenged established societal rules. In the end, that is political. It may not organize itself into a political party, but it is a protest and an alternative way of life. It is a strong protest, given that it is delivered by Jesus, a respected and increasingly influential rabbi.

The symbol of Christ's reign is not the sword of a conqueror, but the towel of a servant. This simple and yet powerful symbol of Christ is usually ignored. We cannot envision a towel as the grand emblem of a ruling kingdom.

Neither was Jesus what the religious leaders expected. Keeping the law had become the icon, the fetish, the idol of the religion of legalism. Moses had brought the first law—the Ten Commandments; Jesus, who said he had come to fulfill the law, was different from Moses. He wrote nothing. Instead, he announced that the law would be written on their hearts. Kingdom behaviour was to work out of the spirit of the law and not to be bound by the letter of the law, as religious leaders supposed. For Jesus, hating a person was every bit as much a violation of the law as was killing.

At the deepest part of their misunderstanding was the kingdom's role in affecting life. Instead of a sword, Jesus offered forgiveness; pushing aside legalism, Jesus offered reconciliation; stepping aside as the conquering hero, Jesus rode on a foal of a donkey; rather than denounce Rome, Jesus allowed soldiers to kill him. Seeming anything but a king, he was the suffering Savior. It was this suffering Savior who would ultimately deal a death blow to the assumption that political influence comes by the power of the sword.

The Encounter with Satan

There is no more explicit example of the mistaken hopes people had for the Messiah than the encounter Jesus had with Satan in the wilderness.

Early in Jesus' earthly ministry, and in preparation for what lay ahead, he went into the wilderness for forty days of prayer and fasting. At the end of this fast, as Jesus was in a weakened condition, Satan appeared and challenged Jesus on three grounds, each representing a primary hope of messiahship. He called Jesus to turn stones into bread. What are most people looking for in a national leader but to be an economic miracle worker? This has become the high-water mark against which we rate our political leaders.

Second, he promised Jesus all the kingdoms of the world if Jesus would bow down and worship him. Power is essential to the world's view of ruling.

Finally, Satan took Jesus to the top of the temple tower in Jerusalem, tempting him to jump. The seduction of this temptation was that by making such a public display, Jesus would verify that indeed he was the Messiah.

Jesus turned down all three, not only to refuse this co-opting by Satan, but to establish the essence of the kingdom.

Those who expected the kingdom of God to burst from the heavens, eradicate the Romans, eliminate hunger, restore justice, and care for the fatherless were bewildered by Jesus' seeming incapacity to deal forcefully with the power-brokers. They failed to understand that the kingdom's work was deeper and farther-reaching than any immediate political solution. Yes, political solutions are important, but at the centre of the human dilemma are self-interest, power, and ego. It was to that concern that Jesus' analysis was addressed.

Kingdom Truth Speaks to Social/Political Realities

In connecting Jesus' life and ministry to what we should do about political life, we often make the mistake of assuming that we should do only what he did. But that would fail to take into account an important difference: Christ's work was to inaugurate and set loose the kingdom; our calling is to interpret and implement. He pushed beyond the limits of Messianic law and underscored that ruling one's spirit was a greater victory than ruling a nation. But he was not saying that the ruling of a nation is not important. It is just that he dug deep into the soil of life and exposed what is deeper and more fundamental, pointing us beyond penultimate values to ultimate ones. By so doing, the kingdom is inclusive and all-encompassing.

Christ's kingdom speaks to our social and political situation in five ways:

1. It is linked to the lessons of Israel's experience.
2. It holds all of life within God's rule.
3. It is transformational.
4. It upsets the assumption of political power.
5. It speaks to the heart of a nation.

1. The message of the kingdom and the suffering Savior is linked to the lessons of Israel's experience

Although the Old Testament did not use the specific term "kingdom," the idea was common among the Hebrew people. Theologian John Bright says it would be clearly understood by the people of Jesus' day:

> The Kingdom of God lay within the vocabulary of every Jew. It was something they understood and longed for desperately. . . . While it underwent . . . a radical mutation on the lips of Jesus, it had a long history and is, in one form or another, ubiquitous in both Old Testament and New. It involves the whole notion of the rule of God over His people, and particularly the vindication of that rule and people in glory at the end of history. That was the Kingdom which the Jews awaited.[2]

Isaiah described that expectation:

> For to us a child is born, to us a son is given, and the govern-

ment will be on his shoulders. And he will be called Wonderful Counselor, Mighty God, Everlasting Father, Prince of Peace. Of the increase of his government and peace there will be no end. He will reign on David's throne and over his kingdom, establishing and upholding it with justice and righteousness from that time on and forever. The zeal of the Lord Almighty will accomplish this (Isa. 9:6, 7).

Throughout the Scriptures there is the constant theme of a Lord who will suffer. While Jesus left no doubt of ultimate authority when he said to Pilate, "Do you think I cannot call on my Father, and he will at once put at my disposal more than twelve legions of angels?" (Matt. 26:53, 54), he recognized the place of suffering (Mark 8:31; 9:12, 31; 10:33, 45).

This suffering and death are in concert with Old Testament references, the most focused being Isaiah 53. The Jewish community understood the suffering Savior (Isaiah 40–66) to be referring to the nation of Israel, not an individual. Jesus turned this around and accepted Isaiah's vision as speaking of himself.

Suffering and death, however, were not to be associated with failure. On that turns the central notion of the kingdom. Success is defined in terms different from those of Rome, and of the temple administrators.

Speaking to the request of James and John to be seated in power with Christ in glory, they were reminded that "even the Son of Man did not come to be served, but to serve, and to give his life as a ransom for many" (Mark 10:45). In Paul's commentary on Isaiah 45:23, the reference to being a servant was not just an idea but a reality:

> But made himself nothing, taking the very nature of a servant, being made in human likeness. And being found in appearance as a man, he humbled himself and became obedient to death— even death on a cross (Phil. 2:7, 8).

For Israel, the idea of a nation had begun with God's call of Abraham. Even though the shift of the Hebrew nation from a theocracy to a monarchy was not God's choice, it was approved. Now that

Jesus had arrived and talked about something quite different from what many expected, they were not sure if it was what they wanted. His talk of the kingdom brought into play a new element. And for Jews being hammered by the Romans, this turning-of-the-other-cheek did not get good play. But Jesus' kingdom would not be bound up in charters, thrones, armies, and treaties, but in God ruling in the thoughts, intents, and actions of people. Christ's kingdom would come by personal and inner rebirth. The role of God in life comes by means of inner power—Jesus told them that a person in control of him- or herself is greater than one who takes a city—something the disciples, after three years under Christ's tutorship, did not understand.

2. The kingdom message includes all of life within its rule

As Jesus stepped onto the pages of history and the Palestinian landscape, he brought an understanding that all of creation and history are part of the kingdom. It was not necessary for Jesus to tell the listeners that. They knew it well.

Today, as inheritors of many forms of political theory and experience, it is important that we strip ourselves of all of that (at least in our attempt to understand what was implicit in the message of Christ's kingdom) and try to hear the message as if we were standing alongside Christ in that day.

In Canada, the act of confederation, the British North America Act of 1867, referred to Psalm 72:8(KJV): "He shall have dominion from sea to sea." As the domain of Canada's rule is everything between the declared boundaries, so Christ's kingdom covers all that exists by creation.

The apostle Paul leaves no doubt about the territory of God's domain:

> For by him all things were created: things in heaven and on earth, visible and invisible, whether thrones or powers or rulers or authorities; all things were created by him and for him. He is before all things, and in him all things hold together (Col. 1:16, 17).

Jesus said, "My kingdom is not of [a better translation is 'from'] this world" (John 18:36). Some Christians interpret this to mean that the kingdom has nothing to do with this world. Not so. Jesus is reminding Pilate that the source of authority for the kingdom is not from the world. But he is not saying the kingdom does not include this world. That makes a world of difference.

Later, when Pilate said, "Do you not realize I have power either to free you or to crucify you?" Jesus replied, "You would have no power over me if it were not given to you from above" (19:10, 11). The issue here concerns the source of authority and power. It is not about whether planet Earth is included under Christ's rule.

The lordship of Christ is affirmed over both heaven and earth. Not only are both God's creation, but in both places the observance of God's will is critical. "Your kingdom come, your will be done on earth as it is in heaven..." (Matt. 6:10) is how Jesus instructs his disciples to pray.

The word "earth" is used in the New Testament in two ways: to describe physical reality—"heaven and earth will pass away" (Matt. 24:35)—and social reality—"You are the salt of the earth" (Matt. 5:13).

The territory of Christ's kingdom goes beyond the physical planet and rulers or governments; it embraces all people. Jesus, replying to the Pharisees who wanted to know when the kingdom would come, said, "The kingdom of God does not come with your careful observation, nor will people say, 'Here it is,' or 'There it is,' because the kingdom of God is within you" (Luke 17:20, 21). What a turn of ideas. Those looking for release from their captors equated the domain of King Jesus with the land boundaries of Palestine.

That he said the kingdom is "within" us was too radical in that it did not take into account the common assumption that a kingdom was primarily political, and therefore required the exercise of power. Jesus exploded that belief by saying that beyond what is physical and obvious to us, there is a terrain that is as real as planet Earth. Speaking to the rich, young man, he challenged him to give up his riches and give the proceeds to the poor "and you will have treasure in heaven" (Mark 10:21).

The kingdom is outside the borders of time. Jesus understood that it is both a present and a future reality. Jesus stood in Israel dur-

ing Rome's rule—a specific location and time. It is also a future reality. "When the Son of Man comes in his glory, and all the angels with
him, he will sit on his throne in heavenly glory" (Matt. 25:31).

The King, in arriving, brought the kingdom. But the fulfillment
and the full influence of the kingdom are being held in suspension.
Hope of what the kingdom will be is still in the future. It is hope that
drives the Christian community forward and gives us encouragement
to live in the most difficult and debilitating of situations.

In its all-inclusiveness, the kingdom extends beyond any particular group or race. Even though the sons and daughters of Abraham
were very conscious of their lineage, Jesus made it clear that such ethnic attachment is not enough to guarantee a place in the kingdom. In
Jesus' opening message in Nazareth (Luke 4), he used illustrations of
two non-Hebrews who responded to God's provisions: a widow in
Sidon supplied with food during a famine, and Naaman, the Syrian
general cured of leprosy. Jesus' message was unmistakable: membership in the kingdom will not be limited to those of a particular clan
or race.

As it was not reserved for those of a race, neither was it for those
who maintained an outward purity, or even those who kept the law.
For if it were, surely the Pharisees would be the first to enter. Jesus
reserved his deepest scorn for them:

> Woe to you, teachers of the law and Pharisees, you hypocrites!
> You are like whitewashed tombs, which look beautiful on the
> outside but on the inside are full of dead men's bones and
> everything unclean (Matt. 23:27).

Unsavory people such as prostitutes, who seemingly had nothing
to offer, were welcomed, while the teachers of the law were excluded
(Matt. 5:20).

Race, status, the meticulous keeping of the law—none of these
qualifies one. Jesus' calling reverberates with what Isaiah heard God say:

> When you come before me ... stop bringing meaningless offer-
> ings! ... They have become a burden to me.... Stop doing
> wrong, learn to do right! Seek justice, encourage the oppressed.

Defend the cause of the fatherless, plead the case of the widow (Isa. 1:12–17).

What could be more out of sync with a Roman-dominated society than the announcement that the new kingdom would be made up of those who are meek and lowly: that its leader is willing to be the last in order to be first and one who models leadership by washing feet? He called the weary ones (Matt. 11:28–30). The wealthy—well, they can come, but wealth is a hindrance, not an asset (Mark 10:17–25). And thieves and prostitutes will make it to the entrance before the religiously upstanding people (Matt. 21:31). This new kingdom will be made up of the social rejects, patently irreligious, financially on the bottom rung: those who know they have nothing to bring but their failures, bankruptcies, broken dreams, and shattered hopes. Paul understood who constituted this strange Kingdom:

Think of what you were when you were called. Not many of you were wise by human standards; not many were influential; not many were of noble birth (1 Cor. 1:26).

This understanding is vital to our application of the relationship of the kingdom to our notion of social/political leadership. Not only does the kingdom hold all things under its rule, but Christ's concern for kingdom rule encompasses groups we might otherwise exclude.

3. The kingdom is transformational

We most easily think of kingdom power as a political, economic, or military power, but Jesus, as Creator, knows the heart and sets about to inaugurate that which will transform instead of adopting the human way—to dominate and control.

Members of the kingdom are those who are ready and prepared to obey. Jesus did not use the law as the gate. He provided another point of entry. Paul described it this way: "Therefore no one will be declared righteous in his sight by observing the law; rather, through the law we become conscious of sin" (Rom. 3:20). Obedience arises not from a desire for religious perfection, but from a willingness to allow Christ to rule one's life—all of it.

The ensuing standards of life then are shaped by what Jesus expects his followers to obey. In the discourse on separating the sheep from the goats, Jesus leaves no doubt what is expected:

> I was hungry and you gave me something to eat, I was thirsty and you gave me something to drink, I was a stranger and you invited me in, I needed clothes and you clothed me, I was sick and you looked after me, I was in prison and you came to visit me (Matt. 25:35, 36).

Thus, although membership in the kingdom does not require obedience to a series of laws, that does not exempt one from right living, or from obedience to the newly defined laws of the kingdom.

Jesus' teaching is a window into the ways of his kingdom. His primary form is storytelling: parables. When asked "Why do you speak to the people in parables?" he replied, "The knowledge of the secrets of the kingdom of heaven [Matthew used "heaven" rather than "God"] has been given to you" (Matt. 13:10, 11).

His "sower" metaphor helps us see both kingdom wisdom and kingdom strategy. He was not depending on military force, or even calling on angelic assistance, but rather was using the power of the Word to call a willing belief and a faithful following. Rome, or Ottawa, can use its political levers to lead, but Christ's kingdom begins at a more fundamental level: at the centre of inner reality, the heart.

Sowing is a gentle and seemingly harmless activity. A seed is dropped into the soil and, in time, brings a harvest. It is hidden from view; it takes time, makes no noise, competes with no one. Nothing threatening here.

It is not just that the words of Christ transform as do ideas of human thought. His words, as seed, are not only revolutionary (although that they are), but life-giving. The seed of the Word actually brings about a release from the chains of human sin and sets in process a new life which grows up within oneself and throughout one's relationships.

Jesus also demonstrated power over the physical realm by the authority of his words. In Capernaum, people "were amazed at his

teaching, because his message had authority." When a man possessed
by a demon recognized him as the Holy One of God, Jesus freed him
(Luke 4:32–36). In the region of the Gadarenes, when Jesus encoun-
tered a man with an evil spirit, there was an immediate recognition of
Jesus' authority (Mark 5:6, 7; cf. Matt. 8:29; Luke 8:28, 31).

The releasing of people from the control of the demonic struck
people as evidence of messiahship. After Jesus had healed and delivered a man, "all the people were astonished and said, 'Could this be
the Son of David?'" (Matt. 12:23).

When the seventy-two of Jesus' disciples returned from their first
mission, they told Jesus what they had seen. Jesus rejoiced with them
and said, "I saw Satan fall like lightning from heaven" (Luke 10:18).
Satan had been defeated. They had seen for themselves that Christ's
kingdom defeated Satan's power.

It may seem strange to include Christ's miracles in a study of the
social/political influence of his kingdom, but they speak to the nature
of it. Nothing is left untouched by Christ's presence, even physical
disabilities. One might say that if Jesus is concerned about a storm in
Galilee, certainly he is interested in the political powers that rule us.

We learn early in Jesus' ministry the strategic importance of
miracles:

> Jesus went through all the towns and villages, teaching in their
> synagogues, preaching the good news of the kingdom and
> healing every disease and sickness (Matt. 9:35).

The working of miracles existed alongside the casting-out of
demons, and preaching as a means of announcing the kingdom. Some
people explain the miracles as being only of that time, or as the workings of a primitive culture. John Bright disagrees:

> He who regards them as an excrescence of the Gospel story, an
> expression of the believers of a superstitious age which must
> be scaled away in order to get back to Jesus as he really was,
> may indeed recover a Jesus palatable to a rationalist intellect—
> but he may be assured that it will not be the Jesus of the New
> Testament faith.[3]

The raising of the dead is also important. The raising of the ruler's daughter (Matt 9:18ff.) and Lazarus (John 11:1ff.) serve not only to etch in the minds of the disciples Christ's true nature, but to identify the nature of the kingdom. The ultimate expression of power is over death. The message is clear: this new kingdom will deal with death in a revolutionary way.

As well as issuing searing words to religious leaders, Jesus cared for a dying woman. This coupling of care for the hurting, speaking to nature, and zeroing in on political strife is consistent with the nature of the kingdom.

Jesus announced the kingdom in the oral tradition of the Middle East—not "words, words and more words," but commands that transform. Luke, the historian, notes, "The Law and the Prophets were proclaimed until John. Since that time, the good news of the kingdom of God is being preached..." (Luke 16:16). The core message is that the kingdom arrives in the preaching of the gospel. *Gospel* and *good news* are used interchangeably. The word *gospel* literally means "joyful news."

Jesus' preaching is unlike others'. His words are beyond rhetoric. They are accompanied by power. He announces truth, which, in and of itself, is transforming. Jesus' healing of a paralytic, and then forgiving his sins, shows the relationship. After the healing, Jesus asked the Pharisees and teachers,

> "Why are you thinking these things in your hearts? Which is easier: to say, 'Your sins are forgiven,' or to say, 'Get up and walk'? But that you may know that the Son of Man has authority on earth to forgive sins...." He said to the paralyzed man, "I tell you, get up, take your mat and go home" (Luke 5:22-24).

Miracles were one thing, but to actually forgive sin?

Because power and authority are clearly a function of Christ's being and mandate, the announced kingdom is filled with all that Jesus is. Such a message is for all people in all times and places. For political leadership unaware of Christ's person, the good news is still a reality. For those of us in lands rich in the history of Christian political engagement, the need to speak again the good news is critical, not only for the benefit that accrues to the political enterprise, but because of the biblical call to speak the good news everywhere.

4. The kingdom overturns our understanding of political power

We assume that the words *political* and *power* go hand in hand. It is true, of course, that one cannot rule a nation without power. Power, in and of itself, is a gift. However, when we use the word *power*, we do so with certain assumptions. We picture a king exercising power by requiring the subjects to obey. In a democratic society we visualize the president or prime minister deciding what will be done because the ruling party has sufficient power—that is, votes—to make the final decision.

The practical question is, how are our political masters able to exercise political leadership? They can lead and exercise political power (meaning influence) only when those over whom they rule give their consent to be governed.

This plays out in everyday life. A teacher, though given the right and task to manage a class, can teach and lead only when the students are willing to recognize his or her authority to teach them. A minister, even though mandated to lead a church, can rule only as the people recognize that authority to lead.

Even in the most onerous of dictatorships, ultimately a ruthless ruler can continue only as long as the people allow it. All the military might in the world will not, in the end, hold the power to rule. Only the authority given by those ruled to those ruling will allow continuing leadership.

When we consider governance, we need not shun political parties or avoid giving leadership; rather, we need to remember that the source of authority is not in the process itself but in God's provision for leadership.

Those who argue that Jesus had no political concern assume that because he did not specifically speak to the issue of Rome, his message was therefore not designed to bring about political change. Indeed, Jesus was a threat to the Roman Empire.

Jesus tells the story about the rich man who built more barns to store his wealth (Luke 12:15–21). His message is not that he broke a law but that in holding on to more possessions than he needs, he is a fool. Here Jesus is attacking the social order of the powerful. Though this might not speak directly to Roman authority, in effect, it does so by disturbing the social order—something Rome was concerned about. If such ideas got popular play in Israel, the ensuing upset would have been politically untenable. His call to the rich young man to sell everything was said in a land where many were poor and only a few were rich.

Jesus' treatment of the oppressed is often missed by some churches who react to a bias often associated with issues of the poor. But such misunderstanding fails to see Jesus' deep concern. When asked by John the Baptist's friends if Jesus really was the Messiah, he said,

> Go back and report to John what you have seen and heard: the blind receive sight, the lame walk . . . and the good news is preached to the poor (Luke 7:22–23).

To a Messiah-awaiting people, the very idea that this Christ (Messiah) would die a death on the cross—the billboard of Roman power—was preposterous. "Just another pseudo-messiah," most would say. The hopes of the disciples and followers were smashed by the collusion of religious and political leaders and the dreaded and hated intruder, Rome. But the mighty Kingdom had come, and Rome's puny efforts could not bring it down. At the very time it seemed all had been lost, all had been won. The cross eventually became a symbol not of tragedy and loss, but of victory and triumph: the power of evil was finally broken. The battle would continue for centuries, but the defeat of evil was certain.

5. Kingdom truth speaks to the heart of a nation

This look at Christ's kingdom sets in context our search for God's will about what is good for my nation and yours, shaped and informed by what Christ meant about our role in fulfilling the prayer, "Your will be done on earth." There are nine factors in this expressed will.

1. Time-oriented: Jesus came in time, which he both created and lived in. He does not trivialize this part of eternity, even though life on earth some day will wind down and be no more.

2. Earth-concerned: As Jesus came in time, he also graced this planet above all others with his body and life. We have no clue as to God's interaction with other planets, or whether life in some form exists there. Earth is more than a vehicle: it is also an expression of God's own creation. Christ's Kingdom, launched here, works out its dynamics within societal living.

3. Engaging darkness: Jesus reminds us that evil is a reality working to disengage creation from its Creator. Jesus' Kingdom is about more than good ideas and integrative truths: it strikes with power at Satan and his kingdom. Facing Satan in the wilderness, the kingdom of God is neither deceived by Satan's lies and seductions nor intimidated by his power.

4. Enacting miracles: The contamination of disease poses no formidable threat to the Creator. Jesus demonstrates to John the Baptist that the kingdom, in facing physical disease and tragedy, brings about healing. In the eye of a storm, Jesus' words bring about atmospheric change. These miracles and others serve to remind us that no matter the wonder or mystery of the physical creation, the kingdom envelops and has power over all.

5. Redefining power: It is here that we see most clearly the central force of Christ's kingdom. Amid the expectation that any kingdom is really about the power to rule, Jesus redefines it. The kingdom way to the throne goes by way of the cross. To rule, one must serve. To become fruitful, one must die; to receive, one must bestow.

6. Encompassing politics: Did Jesus expect Rome to live by his teaching? If he did not call on the disciples to rehabilitate society, then why should we try? The fact is he did, and that rule

covers all of life. It is a rule that begins in the heart of the creation, the human will. Transforming this centre, Christ's kingdom-righteousness overflows to the surrounding world. Just because he did not tell us to build church buildings or run seminaries does not mean we should not do so; nor does it follow that just because he has not called us to be politicians or run grocery stores we should not be politicians or grocers.

7. Recasting leadership: Knowing Christ's recasting of power, we are impressed with the manner in which we are expected to lead. He shows us by example the kingdom-understanding of "lord." We are called to remember the towel. As Messiah, Jesus will lead the people, but in ways that strike confusion in those who know only one way of leading—coercive power. As a servant, Jesus recasts our understanding of kingdom-leading.

8. Requiring ethics: Jesus expected the disciples to take seriously the ethics of the kingdom. While the kingdom is the goal and the reward for those who follow Christ, it is also the means whereby we live out the good news. Our ethics, or moral requirements, are wrapped up in personal obedience to Christ as Lord and Savior. His gospel is not split, divided between personal and social, but rather is unified.

9. Person-centred: Though we want to avoid the Enlightenment ideology of individualism, we see that Jesus gives focus to people. He asks blind Bartimaeus, "What do you want?" He lovingly takes children in his arms. We more clearly understand his person-centredness when we read Paul's description: we are temples of God's Spirit. It is here that God transforms and rewrites on the tablets—or micro-chips—of our hearts the eternal laws. At the same time, we live not to ourselves, but with the community of God's people, the church.

The message of the Kingdom is political. It is not prescriptive in suggesting a political philosophy or structure such as a monarchy or a democracy, but, in calling us to obey God's rule and to live in love with each other, Christ's message is political.

To decide what to do in relation to our political and social setting requires that we weave a garment out of the many threads of Jesus' life, teachings, and ministry. Avoiding formulas or specific instructions, Christ calls us to weave a garment that fits and serves us within the context of our life. By not giving us specifics, kingdom-truth is not bound by era, situation, or political reality. The threads of the kingdom are the same, but the pattern, shape, size, and purpose of the garment will be constructed so that Christ's will in relationship to political life is served.

4

Thinking with a Christian World View

In the previous two chapters we examined the Old and New Testaments for clues to what Christians might believe about their nation, and for insights to guide us in our response to social and political realities.

The Scriptures provide a window through which we look out onto life. In recent decades we have been subjected to a certain perspective or way of seeing: secularism – itself a world view – attempts to screen faith from the public square. That's why it seems difficult to include a Christian point of view in discussions of public policy. For so long, faith has been excluded from such issues that it seems we must live without it. However, while this is at present the status quo of much of political and public life, it does not have to continue to be.

What is required is for Christians to live out their faith, be it in the classroom or in the parliament of their land, by framing all of life within a Christian understanding.

†

One summer, Lily and I spent a couple of weeks in Oxford. I was pleasantly surprised to see the number of colleges with religious names: Jesus College, Trinity College, Christ Church College. But we noted that much of their studies had little reference to their founding spiritual mandates. Their world views were shaped by the secular; that is, God is ignored as a meaningful and knowable reality or object worthy of search.

Harry Blamires, author and colleague of C.S. Lewis, laments,

> We Christians in the modern world accept, for the purpose of mental activity, a frame of reference constructed by the secular mind and a set of criteria reflecting secular evaluations.[1]

To surrender to a non-Christian mindset is to see through lenses that exclude a biblical vision of life.

Thinking Christianly has been discredited by both secularists and Christian sectarians. As secular thinking deprives one's world view of faith as central to understanding life, Christian sectarianism assumes that because the current world is temporary, Christ therefore has little interest in it.

Thinking Christianly is not as easy as it might seem. Contemporary public thought is often biased against a Christian world view. This is Babel at its strongest. Surrounded by groups and communication systems, each broadcasting its own message, we unconsciously or even consciously accept their norms, putting on the glasses of our prevailing culture and seeing life through their lenses. The apostle Paul urges us, "Do not conform any longer to the pattern of this world, but be transformed by the renewing of your mind" (Rom. 12:2).

The prophet Elisha's assistant was frightened as he looked out onto the city and saw the surrounding foreign army. Elisha prayed,

> "Oh Lord, open his eyes so he may see." Then the Lord opened the servant's eyes, and he looked and saw, the hills full

of horses and chariots of fire all around Elisha (2 Kings 6:17).

Elisha didn't panic. Through eyes of faith, he saw more than what his associate saw. This window of faith gave him a broader perspective.

King David, wanting to know the strength of his army, instructed Commander Joab to number the people of Israel (2 Sam. 24:10). Instead of relying on God, David trusted in the strength and size of his army. Turning from trusting God, David instead believed his strength was in the power of armaments and the size of the army. David later noted the futility of basing the idea of winning on his own strength: "Some trust in chariots and some in horses but we trust in the name of the Lord, our God" (Ps. 20:7). "No king is saved by the size of his army; no warrior escapes by his great strength. A horse is a vain hope for deliverance" (33:16, 17). David learned in time that his window was too small.

THREE PARTS OF A CHRISTIAN WORLD VIEW

In learning to think about life within a Christian world view, we must be aware of three important elements in the framework through which to see life: creation, time, and humanity.

Planet Earth

God has not abandoned planet Earth. Creation includes this planet in the universe and, on this planet, humans are made in God's likeness. The physical creation, including distant planets, is part of the grander reality. Though the whole universe will one day be made into a "new heaven and new earth," that does not mean that Earth is without meaning here and now. Indeed, the opposite is true. Created in God's likeness, we inhabit this earth. It was to planet Earth that God's Son came, and it is here that the eternal plan is being worked out. To minimize the importance of Earth is to marginalize the handiwork and plan of God.

David testifies to God's involvement with creation. "The earth is the Lord's and everything in it," he writes; "the world and all who live in it; for he founded it upon the seas and established it upon the waters" (Ps. 24:1). In Psalm 33, the Earth is God's expression of love: "The earth is full of his unfailing love. By the word of the Lord were the heavens made, their starry host by the breath of His mouth." A Hebrew song describes God as the past, present, and future King of the Earth—not as an absentee landlord or a spirit that we can know only after we die: "For God is the King of all the earth. ... God reigns over the nations" (Ps. 47:7-8). This creation is under God's control. "It is I who made the earth, and created mankind upon it. My own hands stretched out the heavens; I marshaled their starry hosts" (Isa. 45:12).

Earth's original human inhabitants received specific instruction in Earth management. After their disobedience, the instruction was to "cultivate the ground from which he was taken" (Gen. 3:23, NASB). This was not punishment, but a continuation of the assignment given to them before the fall (1:28).

Jesus taught the disciples to pray: "Your kingdom come, your will be done on earth as it is in heaven" (Matt. 6:10). The "on earth" of Jesus' prayer directly focuses our attention on God's concerns being worked out where we stand—on this geographical place of our existence. Jesus does not allow us to "spiritualize" his concern as being that of "in the sweet by and by," but holds us in the present tense and in the place where we live. Christians in the early church gave praise for the release of Peter and John. They prayed, "Sovereign Lord, you made the heaven and the earth and the sea and everything in them..." (Acts 4:24). We live with hope for our eternal existence, but until then, as an integral part of the creation, we are called on to enjoy and care for this planet Earth.

Time

God has not abandoned time—it was created, and we are placed within it. We are not just putting in time, waiting until eternity wraps us up. Although we are to "set [our] minds on things above" (Col. 3:2) to establish right motivations, we are not to spend our days indolently dreaming of heaven. Rather, we are called to live out our days as a means of knowing and doing God's will and purposes. As a colleague said, time is when the genetic code for eternity is being written. Earth is not everything, and time is not all there is, but they are God's creation; they are both preparatory and preliminary to all of the very best there is and will be.

As we moved from one millennium into the next, there was an enormous interest in "End Time" ideas. Jesus warned us not to be unduly preoccupied by the exact time of his return. Speaking of the coming of the "Son of Man," he warned,

> No one knows about that day or hour, not even the angels in heaven, nor the Son, but only the Father. Be on guard! Be alert! You do not know when that time will come (Mark 13:32, 33).

Our life is not to be squandered; we are to use it both to manage the Earth and to prepare for Christ's return. Paul reminds us to use time well:

> And do this, understanding the present time. The hour has come for you to wake up from your slumber, because our salvation is nearer now than when we first believed. The night is nearly over; the day is almost here. So let us put aside the deeds of darkness and put on the armor of light (Rom. 13:11, 12).

Humanity

In spite of sin, which spoils all creation, God has not abandoned us. Though Earth and time are part of creation, we are God's special creation. Made "in his own image" (Gen. 1:27), humanity has the unique and awesome responsibility of bearing God's image in life. Even though humanity lives in rebellion, we have opportunity to know God. While the life of the Spirit and life of the world are in tension, Jesus gives us an opportunity to enter into life prepared for creation.

The entry of evil into earthly life changed the nature of creation and the workings of human motivations. This reality did not set aside God's interest or plan to have fellowship with the creation. For in the midst of human history, with our failures and proclivity toward self-interest, God had a plan centred in Jesus Christ. Given that humans are a special creation, the freeing of humans from the bondage of evil was intrinsic to God's overall agenda.

Yes, people do matter. We are given the task of carrying on the kingdom. What is astounding and distinctive about Christian faith is that those who turn to Christ become the habitat of God's life. "Do you not know that your body is a temple of the Holy Spirit, who is in you, whom you have received from God?" the apostle Paul asks. Why else would there be the constant reminder that our bodies are to be kept to honour God? Paul concludes, "You are not your own; you were bought at a price. Therefore honour God with your body" (1 Cor. 6:19, 20).

Jesus' famous line leaves no doubt of his commitment to people: "For God so loved the world that he gave his one and only Son..." (John 3:16). Even in discipline, God's concern is shown. "When we are judged by the Lord," Paul writes, "we are being disciplined so that we will not be condemned with the world" (1 Cor. 11:32). Even though evil works to destroy, it will never succeed, for it is God who protects and controls our destinies. Again Paul writes, "For by him all things were created: things in heaven and on earth, visible and invisible, whether thrones or powers or rulers or authorities; all things were created by him and for him" (Col. 1:16).

> For I am convinced that neither death nor life, neither angels nor demons, neither the present nor the future, nor any powers, neither height nor depth, nor anything else in all creation, will be able to separate us from the love of God that is in Christ Jesus our Lord (Rom. 8:38, 39).

It is not possible to overstate our importance to God. We do not know what exists on other planets of the galaxies, but we do know that on planet Earth, God invested the life of the Son so that by Christ's death and resurrection we, too, can know eternal life.

FINDING A NATIONHOOD VISION—DOES MY COUNTRY MATTER?

Does God's concern for humanity mean God has a particular concern for communities or nations? Does God care specifically about

Canada or Ghana or Sri Lanka? Does the Bible say anywhere that God is concerned with a nation as such? To put it another way, does nationhood, as a category of human existence, have any place in the plans of God? Can there be, for the Christian, such a thing as a biblical vision for one's nation?

Some people are made nervous by such talk, and for good reason. Church and political leaders have too often used religion as a means of exercising power. Christians do not want to make national situations worse by embracing a simplistic or otherwise unsound biblical view of their country. Most Christians would reject the view that their country has been especially chosen by God above other nations.

Overdramatization is not necessary. We examine the Scriptures to see what might be God's concern for a nation. To develop an appropriate biblical model for one country, it is not enough to collect a few pithy Bible verses, mix them together with our religious past, and say, "Here's the answer."

The Bible does not let us get away with such narrow or shallow thinking. "The whole counsel of God" does not mean bits and pieces, "sound bites," or one-dimensional pictures. In approaching any controversial question, we need to "correctly handle the word of truth" (2 Tim. 2:15). The Christian world view is not made up of a series of slogans designed to address the problems of the day and posited as some sort of cure-all. It comes out of the Hebrew community's long struggle. It is epitomized in Jesus' teachings about his kingdom. And it has been demonstrated in many forms through the continuing development of the church throughout its 2,000-year sojourn.

If we fail to look at the big picture, if we avoid struggling with the issues of Christian faith and action, the consequences could be monstrous. Working on the assumption that our nation and the way we relate to it are of concern to God, if we do not engage, we end up being unfaithful both to our nation and to the Lord we serve.

WHY SHOULD WE CARE?

For some Christians a nagging question remains: Given God's promise of eternity, is there any reason why a Christian should be concerned about the social and political structures of today? Often a person who asks this assumes that aspects of Christ's kingdom—including conversion, life in the Spirit, the coming of Christ, the future new heavens and earth—have nothing to do with our country. The question could be phrased another way: "Do our beliefs and actions have consequence only insofar as they affect eternal matters?" If the answer is yes, then any other concern about life is at best secondary, but not compelling. Such a view leads to four faulty conclusions.

The first is that the state exists without any legitimate essence of its own. That is, God uses this part of creation only for something else: as if it doesn't have meaning in and of itself. But this runs contrary to Paul's assertion that

> by him all things were created: things in heaven and on earth, visible and invisible, whether thrones or powers or rulers or authorities; all things were created by him and for him (Col. 1:16, 17).

Second, if the state does not bring glory to God, it falls into the category of "necessary evil," without any legitimacy as a creation of God. However, such a conclusion forces us to ignore the Scriptures, which speak of political concerns. Richard Mouw, president of Fuller Theological Seminary, writes,

> God's promise to bless the descendants of Abraham included references to their political well-being; when the Israelites were rescued out of Egypt, the bonds of their political oppression had to be broken; the psalmists wrote political prayers; the prophets delivered messages about political policies; Jesus faced political temptations; apocalyptic visions include political scenarios.[2]

If the state is a necessary evil, it would follow that it would be counterproductive for Christians not only to engage in any aspect of state activities—including teaching school or working as a forest ranger—but to care at all about our society or the environment would only serve the source of evil.

Third, by asserting that the state is without value, we end up saying that the significance of human institutions—and the individuals

who work in them—can be determined only by what they will produce in eternity. It is as if our present life has nothing to do with our
future; as though our inner life is disembodied from what is around
us. Thus, as long as I am good on the "inside," this false view concludes, I have fulfilled my responsibilities as a Christian. James, a disciple and New Testament writer, had something to say about that:

> What good is it, my brothers, if a man claims to have faith but
> has no deeds? Can such faith save him? Suppose a brother or
> sister is without clothes and daily food. If one of you says to
> him, "Go, I wish you well; keep warm and well fed," but does
> nothing about his physical needs, what good is it? In the same
> way, faith by itself, if it is not accompanied by action, is dead
> (2:14–17).

The false separation of Spirit life from life in Christ's creation leads
to spiritual schizophrenia and the age-old heresy of Gnosticism. Some
seeking inner spirituality discount the earth as being of concern to
God and deny material reality as a legitimate part of God's kingdom.

Gnostic teachers made a distinction between the *Demiurge* (seen
by ancient Greeks as an inferior deity, responsible for creating the
material world) and the unknowable Divine Being. Into some humans
entered the spark of Divine substance, and by means of *gnosis* (intu-
itive knowledge), they would be rescued from the material world and
brought back into the world of the Divine. Material reality was therefore seen as evil. For them, Jesus Christ could not be incarnate, for that
would have meant the combining of the Divine Being with the material. To a Gnostic, Jesus did not have a material body, but simply took
the façade of a mortal. Those who opposed this teaching emphasized
the actual hand of God in creation; the goodness of material reality;
and the literal physical existence, and the bodily life, death, and resurrection of Jesus Christ.

Some Christians who deny that issues of public life are important
to a Christian world view are, on the other hand, successful in accu-
mulating wealth or getting an education. Some who contend that
their only concern is to prepare people for eternity build and maintain expensive buildings, and have salaried staff and large budgets to

serve the many needs of their members, which, in effect, contradicts their view of God as being concerned only with eternity. At stake in this discussion is not whether these church activities are legitimate, but whether the importance invested in them is consistent with one's views of involvement in public life.

Fourth, by claiming that a nation is outside God's agenda, we unwittingly say that the ethics of Christ's kingdom have no application to public affairs. This precludes anyone, Christian or a believer in another faith, from calling on government to be accountable to the Creator and to act in just and merciful ways. Truth, then, is relative, applying only to Christians. It denies that God is God of all.

These four conclusions point out the fallacy of assuming a nation has no place in Christ's concern. Also if we work outside of a rigourous biblical framework, we can be trapped by excessive nationalism—caught up in blindly believing that one's nation is closest to God's heart; by debilitating anxiety—fear that God has no concern for one's national habitation; or by corrosive cynicism—a complete discounting of any possibility of God's intervention into the affairs of state.

ISRAEL: A LIGHT TO THE NATIONS

The story of Israel is helpful in this context, for it speaks of God's mind for a nation. The Hebrews were called out as a people and given specific parameters within which to live. We can then take the stories, promises, and characters of their story and see how they might apply to our lives. The proclivities of raw and ruthless characters such as Cain and Samson become warnings to our youth. David's songs become grist for sermons on hope. Prophetic thunderings become the stuff of cultural analysis. Dipping into this reservoir is too much to resist.

As we consider the shaping of ideas for one's own country, there are two dangers: to take God's promises to Israel and, without careful biblical study, make them promises to us; and to avoid Israel altogether for fear some misguided nationalist might apply God's treatment of Israel directly to the United States or Canada, claim "chosen" status for the country, and justify all sorts of power-mongering in the name of the will of God.

Such fears are well-founded. Political errors have been made in the past. That does not mean we should give up searching for appropriate ways to apply these lessons. To keep us from that trap, there are a few "don'ts" to keep in mind:[3]

1. *Don't* pick up a promise from Israel, pull it into today's situation, and automatically assume the very same should or will apply today. Principles may be learned from the promise, but the promise may not be strictly applicable in the way it may first appear.

2. *Don't* assume that your country is Israel, and that therefore what God did with that nation is true for yours. Your history is different, and so is your calling. God called the nation of Israel to a specific geographical area and promised certain things for them.

3. *Don't* assume that the Bible gives us a precise blueprint. The Bible describes what was said and what happened, and from that we learn principles of personal and national life. As we read of Israel's formation, its coming of age in the promised land, and God's use of surrounding nations to teach Israel lessons, a pattern gradually forms.

Two examples of abuse of national visions based on misinterpretations of the Scriptures come to mind. Central to the founding of the United States was the idea of "manifest destiny." There was an assumption that God had especially called America into being and had manifested a particular destiny for the nation—that is, to be the "Israel" of the new world. American sociologist Seymour Lipset, in analyzing this fallacy, writes, "The United States is seen as the new Israel." Quoting Robert N. Bellah, he continues,

> Europe is Egypt; America the promised land. God has led His people to establish a new sort of social order that shall be a light to all nations.[4]

It is healthy to hold one's own nation in high regard, but the use of God's call to Abraham and the subsequent forming of Israel as a parallel to the creation of the United States can lead to all sorts of excesses. For example, some defend the build-up of military power on the basis that, as God's chosen land, the United States is called to defend biblical values. There may be sound reasons for a strong military, but to base one's rationale on being the chosen nation to defend God's interests is a distortion, and is very dangerous.

The Boers also abused their knowledge of God's covenant with Abraham in equating their takeover of South Africa with Israel's conquering of Palestine. The laws of apartheid rose out of this misapplication of the Hebraic model. South African church statesman Michael Cassidy describes the distorted nationalism that arose from those scriptural misinterpretations:

> This leads us to what is perhaps the greatest problem which South African nationalisms raise for evangelism, namely the clash between the relative ethic of nationalism and the absolute ethic of Christianity. ...[S]ome African nationalisms, assuming a semi-religious dimension and defining their own ethical absolutes, begin to equate their own political process with the divine will.[5]

So how do we fairly use Israel as a model or example? One helpful way is to see Israel as "a light to the nations." That light, as we know, almost went out. But we have a record of that light as a clue, a direction, an idea. We can learn from its history, its mistakes, failures and successes. When we read the history of Israel, we are listening in on an extraordinary dialogue. The constant interplay between God and this people gives us an idea of what countries should and should not do, and shows us the concerns, expectations, and judgments of God.

In examining the history of Israel, there are guidelines to keep us from misapplying Israel's experience. First, Israel had a special place in the plan and economy of God. Abraham did not just happen to leave his homeland and venture into new territory. The design was to establish a nation through which God's salvation would come to the entire world. This semi-nomadic Semitic tribe was different from all other tribes and nations. Founders of new nations cannot assume that God will rubber-stamp their future plans just because of this promise to Abraham.

Second, the biblical record shows Israel growing into nationhood. For a good part of its history, Israel was an assembly of primitive Middle Eastern tribes traveling to Canaan, then wandering in the wilderness after their escape from Egypt—a far cry from most of today's nations, with their set boundaries. The story of its experience is just that—a story. We listen and watch as they fumble along, failing God, caught up in their own peculiar cultural problems, from time to time showing a flash of obedience and cultural genius. At the beginning, they had no land of their own. And once they did claim what God had promised them, they were frequently invaded and carried off into other lands, forced to live as exiles.

As desert tribes with a relatively short history they were, ethnically speaking, a homogeneous people who traced their roots to Abraham. They were instructed to protect their distinct language, history, and faith from contamination by other cultures and religions because they had a peculiar reason for being made a nation. No other nation would ever fall heir to the promise of being the cradle of God's Son; nor would any other nation ever be as clearly God-directed as Israel. Their history could not be written for any other peoples or nations. Their nation was unique, without parallel, and not to be seen again.

The Hebrews' understanding of God came from observing God at work. They did not think in philosophical categories, as did the Greeks. They did not work from a plan or blueprint. They determined their future actions by remembering God's leading in the past and by recalling what God had done.

WORLDLINESS

Now a word about a problem that has kept many Christians from seriously considering tackling concerns and issues in the broader society. The word most often used is *worldliness*.

I was raised in a church community that defined certain behaviors as "worldly." One such behaviour was smoking. Because of its addictive properties (we did not then understand its relationship to one's health), smoking was associated with being unwilling to submit to the Lordship of Christ. Another "worldly" activity was drinking alcohol, which was seen as a cause of many of society's ills.

In much the same way, some Christians viewed engagement in public activity as a violation of the call to "come out from them and be separate, says the Lord. Touch no unclean thing, and I will receive you" (2 Cor. 6:17). Concern for national/political issues was seen as wandering too close to worldliness.

We must take seriously this concern of "being in the world, but not of the world." To get at it, we need to see it through a Christian world view. First we examine what "the world" does not mean, and then construct a working definition.

What It Is Not

"Worldliness" does not refer to the physical world. Planet Earth is God's creation. "The earth is full of his unfailing love" (Ps. 33:5). When it was created, God looked at it and said, "It is good." Subsequent to creation, sin entered into all of human life, which includes the earth. But that is not to say that the earth and its products are "worldly."

"Worldliness" does not refer to the physical body. Made in God's image, the human body, though infected by sinfulness, is the handiwork of God's creation. John shocked those who believed the body was evil when he said, "The Word [Jesus] became flesh and made his dwelling among us" (John 1:14). Paul went so far as to remind us that our bodies are "temples" of God (1 Cor. 3:16). God takes up residence in this physical construct.

Neither does "worldliness" mean the act of living in the world. It is in the world that we encounter the life of Jesus. The drama of God's recreating life is played out on the stage of life, in this world.

Using one's gifts is not synonymous with "worldliness." Gifts and abilities are part of God's creation. At the very core of our being is a calling to live by making use of these gifts. To own and use our gifts is to fulfill our calling.

Thus, "worldliness" is not synonymous with the Earth, physical life, human experience, or abilities.

A Working Definition

So what do we mean by "worldliness"? It is giving preferred status to something other than God, setting up anything in life above devotion and obedience to God. When Moses was receiving the Ten Commandments and absent from the people, his brother Aaron crafted a golden calf, an object for the people to worship. The golden calf became a symbol for worship over the Creator, making it an idol.

"Worldliness" means allowing other concerns to overcome faith. It was "by faith" that Abraham heard and obeyed the voice of God. He understood this to be the most central aspect of walking with God. We are called to base all of life on the belief that God meant what he said and that our very lives are to be lived according to his Word.

"Worldliness" is also to live without regard to eternity, absorbed with storing wealth and gaining fame without any thought to how one will spend eternity. Because we are people of time, that is the only construct we really understand. Entering into adulthood, we chart a course that follows in line with whatever we believe is important. This is valid and appropriate. But it should not be all; we will live on into eternity. Not to compute eternity into the equation of what I do today is to miss a vital element of the kingdom. If I do not respect my ultimate destination, life becomes worldly.

"Worldliness" is also to live outside of issues or matters that concern God. We don't have a simple listing, but the Scriptures faithfully record God's call. The Israelites were told what was required: "To do justice, to show mercy and to walk humbly before their God"—reinforced by Jesus in Matthew 23:23. If, for example, in running a business our concerns are focused only on the "bottom line" and God's concerns—such as just treatment of employees—are ignored, that business is worldly.

Having a worldly spirit is to put oneself over others. The drive to be profitable, if it is at the expense of others, is "worldliness." Success is not the antithesis of a God-centred life. But in all aspects of living, we are called to "love your enemies and pray for those who persecute you" (Matt. 5:43-44). If getting ahead requires that I step on others, my profit has become rooted in worldliness.

"Worldliness" means preoccupation with religious correctness. In Jesus' day, it was the Pharisees who occupied this ground. Today, those of the religious left and right can be accused equally of having such a preoccupation. If holding onto my faith means intolerance of those with whom I disagree, that faith can itself be overcome by a worldly spirit. For example, a public stand on moral issues often leads to strongly expressed views by various sides. If, in the debate, a Christian is caught in personal recriminations, that is far from Christ's way. Firm convictions are important, and disagreement is expected, but the Spirit never bears the fruit of intolerance.

At its heart, "worldliness" overrides God's concern, which is the agenda of the King. The Sermon on the Mount is explicit, definitive, and all-encompassing. One just needs to ask oneself, "What would be the concern and action plan of Jesus in this situation?" If my attitudes, aspirations, behaviour and relationships are not in line with the concerns of Christ's kingdom, that is "worldliness."

WORLD VIEW AS STRATEGY

A well-developed and thoughtful world view is critical in developing a strategy for engaging our culture. By understanding that the earth, time, people, and our work are part of God's concern, we can understand our activities to be spiritual in the deepest sense, which, in turn, reminds us that we are about eternal realities, and that our work is accountable to our Creator. We further understand that the political state is not necessarily in opposition to God's purposes, and that God's agenda can be furthered by Christian people's engaging in service to the state. This is in no way to give up the exclusive call to love only God, nor is it to assume that caring for our society means we buy into cultural assumptions. Our calling is not just to make this a better world in which to live. Nor should our politics determine our faith.

As disciples of Christ, we ask the tough questions and seek to honour Christ in all we do. Operating out of that biblical world view, we are careful to employ the metaphor of Israel and seek to be guided by lessons and insights gained out of this unique calling.

5

Lessons from the Past: Christians and Rome

This generation is not the first to wonder how their Christian faith relates to the ruling authorities. This conundrum has existed from the time of the earliest Christian communities. The challenge is made more complex by four countries that have been greatly influenced by Christian faith, but in recent years have moved to exclude faith from the public square.

Beginning in Constantine's Rome, Christians have struggled with linking church to political reign. For 2,000 years the church has tried to make sense of the relationship it should have with the political centre. In this chapter, working our way through the Holy Roman Empire to the Reformers and Radical Evangelicals, we examine the various models.

✝

Some Christians object to their colleagues getting involved in political leadership. They argue that too easily they can be drawn into a love for power or be subverted by worldly thinking. That, indeed, is a danger. History is replete with illustrations that underscore such concerns. The counterforce to the subtle and powerful magnet of wanting political power is to maintain a prophetic distance; that is, to be able to say, on any issue, "This is what God says." A tension between being engaged and retaining objectivity is essential.

The danger of being compromised by holding power, however, does not eliminate the importance of God's love for the whole world—"God so loved the world..." Each human is imprinted with the image of God and is of such inestimable worth that God "gave his one and only Son..." (John 3:16). All of politics, notwithstanding its dangers, is subsumed under this reality.

As we explore the relationship of church and state, we note that although individuals and governments are both part of God's creation, only people participate in the eternal kingdom. Eternity is the privilege of the person, not of social systems.

Even so, while only the individual is made in the image of God (Gen. 1:27), the government is also God's creation (Col. 1:16). There is, as political scientist Glenn Tinder notes, an

> ambiguity of our political obligations. If we recognize what God has done—so Christian principles imply—we shall be limitlessly respectful of human beings but wary of society.[1]

POLITICAL DISTINCTION

As God's special creation, we live in the world and its various social constructs. Yet we are wary of their inherent sinful inclinations. The political order, clearly designed to serve the social needs of humanity (Rom. 13), is maintained and influenced by humanity, the fallen. That is why we are to be wary. This wariness is the prophetic distance—not a barrier, but rather a perspective that reminds us of the tension between the knowledge of light and the knowledge of darkness. There is a difference between integrating faith with all of life—including politics—and making it appear that one's particular political view is the only one that can be seen as "Christian."

The role of the prophet is to help us understand what it means to live as citizens of God's eternal kingdom while being good citizens. We participate in public leadership, not because we believe that only Christ's followers have answers (for all truth is God's truth), but in response to the call to "occupy" (Luke 19:13 KJV) until the Master returns. (In this parable, the noble man, before he goes on a long journey, gave his servants money and told them to make good on this investment until he returned.) We offer our resources, not with the view that we have more than others, but with the knowledge that what we have under God's blessing is multiplied, as happened with the young lad who gave his meager lunch not to the crowds but to Jesus, who, in turn, supplied the meal to the crowds. As distance is a characteristic of the prophet, so is humility.

There is an appropriate reserve that should characterize a Christian's relationship to societal activity. Uncritical nationalism wraps its flag around the gospel. Emotional patriotism and chest-thumping confidence blind the eye to self-centred policies and activities. Paul, in reminding Christians in Corinth about the shortage of time, says, "For this world in its present form is passing away" (1 Cor. 7:31). Take the world seriously, but not so seriously that it is seen as the only reality.

The prophetic stance also sees each political movement with a critical eye, looking down the road with a hope in what will be. In seeing beyond the current moment, we are reminded of God's promise. The kingdom is here; it is at work; it will come in its fullness. Beyond the cyclical view of reincarnation or the hopelessness of nihilism, Christian engagement is reinforced by an understanding that God has both a plan and an order. For Christians in the first century, befuddled by the rampant worldliness of the church in Corinth, the apostle John's revelation of the future gives hope (Rev. 1:7, 8). Out of this conviction of God's current activity and hope in future reality, we work at bringing civility and goodness to our neighbours and society.

Some question that if Jesus and the disciples showed such little interest in their surrounding social and political order, what business do we have in being concerned about our nation today? Jesus had a very specific focus: to announce the arrival of the kingdom. His stated agenda lacked specifics, but the outworking of his message had enormous political impact. There were many things about which Jesus had little to say. For example, not much is said about the church. Only three times does Matthew record Jesus even using the word "church," and the other writers of the Gospels never mention it. Yet, Christ's coming founded the church. The point is that Jesus focused on setting out the essence and presence of the kingdom and simply did not give details. However, this is not to say his life did not have profound political influence, as I'll note later.

THE RELATIONSHIP OF THE EARLY CHURCH AND ROME

During its early years, it seems that church authorities showed no interest in reforming Rome. They did hear the mandate of Christ to go into all the world and preach the gospel, and did so to the point of death. It is evident that they were making an impact: "Look, those who have turned the world upside down are come hither also" (Acts 17:6 KJV). But there was no indication that the ruling powers were of any interest to them. It was not because the Romans were a defeated people; instead, there seemed to be joy in accepting the condemnation from their detractors. Stephen looked into the face of Jesus as he died. There was no sense of defeat or reluctance to go anywhere for their King.

The launching of Christ's kingdom occurred in a time when Rome was at the apex of her political power, and the Greek culture of Hellenism was spread throughout the known world. A little band of people known as Christians and considered to be members of a Jewish sect, were called on, by the nature of their faith, to live out their belief system in a world smug with its own military might and determined that those who lived under its political canopy were to give allegiance to none other than Caesar. Christians refused, and therein lies the essence of the story of the tragedy and heroism of Christians in Rome up to the fourth century A.D.

The politics of Rome was built on the view that the state was supreme. Increasingly the state was deified because Caesar, as its head, was seen as an association with deity. Within the pomp and ceremony of this nationalism, all were expected to put the veneration of the state above individual faith. Thus, allegiance to Rome was mandatory. For the Christian, such a view of the state was nothing less than idolatrous. It was at this point that the two kingdoms clashed.

In reflecting on the church of that era, keep in mind that today the church represents the status quo. In the European and North American communities, for hundreds of years the church was either close to or at the centre of power. But in the early days of the church, it was revolutionary. The disciples were accused of "turning the world upside down." Christians were often seen as subversive to the Roman government because their allegiance to Christ was all-inclusive. Though Rome may have lumped Christians together with the many cults of that day, it is clear that Rome was offended, if not threatened, by the worshiping of Jesus of Nazareth.

The historian Tertullian, an African church father (AD 160–225), in commenting on the way pagan Rome blamed them for all of its problems, said the pagans

> take the Christians to be the cause of every disaster to the State, of every misfortune of the people. If the Tiber reaches the walls, if the Nile does not rise to the fields, if the sky doesn't move or the earth does, if there is famine, if there is plague, the cry is at once: "The Christians to the lions."[2]

It was not so much a perceived Christian association with political unrest that seemed to confuse Rome as the way Christians lived, and their refusal to accept the primacy of Roman gods. The Christians could have had their own beliefs as well, but it was their exclusivity that affronted the Romans, who thought that their own gods were insulted. Rome was understandably confused by this religious sect.

An Epistle to Diognetus, written by an unknown writer around AD 150, says:

The Christians are distinguished from other men neither by
country, nor language, nor the customs which they observe.
For they neither inhabit cities of their own, nor employ a peculiar form of speech, nor lead a life which is marked out by any
singularity. ...They dwell in their own countries, but simply as
sojourners. As citizens, they share in all things with others, and
yet endure all things as sojourners. Every foreign land is to
them as their native country, and every land of their birth as a
land of strangers. ...They are in the flesh, but they do not live
after the flesh. They pass their days on earth, but they are citizens of heaven. They obey the prescribed laws, and at the same
time surpass the laws by their lives. They love all men, and are
persecuted by all. ...They are poor, yet make many rich. ...To
sum up all in one word—what the soul is in the body, that are
Christians in the world.[3]

Christians felt that the Bible called on them to give honour to the
government as it acted under God's authority. Paul makes this assertion:

Everyone must submit himself to the governing authorities, for
there is no authority except that which God has established.
...For he is God's servant to do you good (Rom. 13:1, 4).

Christians asserted that they could not recognize Rome as
supreme. So they were persecuted, not because they had a specific
faith, but because they refused to say, "We have no king but Caesar."
    Religion in Rome was not a private affair; it was intimately tied
up with public life. Sacrifice, which was at the heart of ancient Roman
ritual, was paid for by the state. The city, led by state officials, was
absorbed by religious pagan celebrations. Note Acts 19, at Ephesus, in
which the town clerk dismissed a rioting mob who thought the riot
was some sort of meeting held in honour of a pagan god.
    There was no consistent pattern of treatment of the Christians by
the Romans during the first three centuries, but because Christians
refused to be part of pagan worship, they were noticed. As well, by living a life that the Romans viewed as being unnecessarily puritanical,
they stood out. They simply could not live their faith in a concealed

way. While it seemed to others that they were being antisocial by avoiding the public celebrations and ceremonies, they stayed away because of the association with pagan gods. This was interpreted by the Romans as a boycott.

Although Christians avoided any kind of public involvement, their witness was not silenced. Celsus, the pagan pamphleteer, complained that Christian faith was showing up in pagan households. It also found its way into the army and into Caesar's household.[4] But what was its relationship to the state during this early period?

While there were periods in which martyrdom was the norm, Oxford scholar T.M. Parker warns us not to imagine that the tension between the Roman authorities and Christians was a conspiracy.

> Rather it was a fight between the State on the one hand and, on the other, an organization which defended itself by endurance, by apologetic, by open challenge or by other public means short of armed resistance, going partially underground only when no other course was possible and never for long.[5]

Up to the time of Nero, Christianity was not seen as unlawful. Following the fire in Rome, Nero took out his vengeance on Christians, but their treatment was not consistent or continuous. They were a marked people however, given their refusal to participate in public religious ritual. Rumours quickly circulated, especially during times of difficulty, much as they did against Jews in Europe in the early twentieth century.

As well, Christians had no protection in law; that is, they did not have the right to live freely. Roman law did not operate on the premise that citizens could live freely as long as they observed what the law forbade. In Rome, the opposite was true: If apprehended by the authorities, an individual was held responsible for citing laws that supported his or her questioned behaviour or actions. Under this system, judges had wide discretionary powers. Thus, an anti-Christian, state-directed assault was possible, even though there was no law prohibiting Christian worship. It seemed that persecution was most often carried on by roving bands devoted to wreaking havoc on those who, by refusing to worship Roman gods, were seen as atheists.

How did Christians respond? Parker notes two ways. First, they viewed political powers as being ordained by God. They saw the unfortunate mistakes of the Empire as attributable to Rome's failure to understand that Christians make the most loyal citizens. Even though, as Christians, they could not worship Caesar, they did pray for him and believed that the Roman Empire was a force for good. And when persecuted, they prayed for the conversion of their persecutors. Parker refers to a passage in the "Epistle to Diognetus," written in the Apostolic Age, which makes a comparison between the soul of the world and the Christian community. It holds high a view that respects human society, in which Christians are called to preserve natural morality. The writer acknowledges that "they are not of the world," but adds that their calling to exercise good influence on the world is their "highest order."[6]

The second way some Christians responded was by taking a more apocalyptic view: they saw the Roman Empire as demonic, opposing Christ's kingdom. Since most writers of this early period were better educated, the received wisdom reflected the view of Diognetus. However, Hermas did not concur with this view. A writer from the less-educated community, he took up the apocalyptic theme of the end of the age:

> The black is this world in which ye dwell; and the fire and blood color showeth that this world must perish by blood and fire; and the golden part are ye that have escaped from this world. ...But the white portion is the coming age, in which the elect of God shall dwell.[7]

Christians of both views shared a contempt for the pagan gods and rituals of Roman life. The pagan gods were not just fancy names for ceremony, but demonic personages who tricked people. An empire that worshiped such demons could only be an enemy of their God. Tertullian, grieved by the open paganism, prayed for the political leaders. His perception of Roman leadership was clear:

> We must needs respect the Emperor as the chosen of the Lord, so that I might say Caesar is more ours than yours, appointed as he is by our God.[8]

Christians, in his view, had good reason for such prayers. If the Empire suffered, Christians, in turn, would suffer, so best pray for the emperors and the entire Empire. He offers this reason:

> We know that the great force which threatens the whole world, the end of the age itself with its menace of hideous suffering, is delayed by the respite which the Roman Empire means for us. We do not want to experience all that; and when we pray for its postponement we are helping forward the continuance of Rome.[9]

To Tertullian, Rome was just a moment in the plan of God, but a moment not to be seen as irrelevant.

> A Christian is the enemy of no man, least of all the Emperor: knowing that he is set up by his own God, he must needs love him, reverence, honour and wish him well, together with the whole Roman Empire, as long as this age endures. For so long shall it endure.[10]

Rome was God's means of holding society together until the End came.

The church, even under persecution, was making inroads into the Empire. Even before a new edict by Constantine in the fourth century, Christians owned buildings that housed their churches. Their leaders increasingly influenced the Roman community. As the third century drew to a close, the hostility and antagonism toward Christians by the Roman state were not strong.

CHRISTENDOM

In AD 306, in a Roman army outpost in Britain, Constantius Chlorus, chief emperor in the west, died, and his son, Constantine, was proclaimed successor. After a number of key battles, in 324 he became sole emperor of the Roman Empire.

This young Roman soldier, now emperor, brought enormous changes in the relationship of the church and the state. In the battle of the Milvian Bridge over the Tiber in Rome, in 312, on his way to becoming emperor, Constantine adopted the Christian insignia for his army. (Some suggest that in a moment of anxiety before the battle, he called on the God of his Christian wife.) Under the aegis of the Edict of Milan, Christianity was given legal status and, in AD 381, made the official religion. The church, formally sanctioned by the political ruler, now received special privileges. This idea of a Christian state was new and radical to the experience of the early Christians.

This began the era in which the church would learn to use political power in inaugurating the kingdom; it would last until Martin Luther nailed a set of propositions to the Wittenberg church door in Germany in 1517. Once the church had gained political influence, the longing for Christ to return and set up the kingdom was modified because now the church had political power to bring in the kingdom. The driving expectation of Christ's return faded. No longer did desperate life circumstances force Christians to rely on the hope of the immediate return of Christ. The blessings of martyrdom in the Coliseum in earlier times as a glorious entry into heaven were no more. The vision had changed. Now it focused on the rule of all of society; the goal was to Christianize it and, by so doing, ensure that Christ's rule commanded all areas of society.

Constantine, in his leadership, was careful not to upset the pagan presence and rituals with this new Christian presence. In AD 313 a Roman medallion was struck. It portrayed the emperor in his helmet, the she-wolf of Roman paganism on his shield, and a cruciform sceptre in his hands—an example of his skill in keeping all sides happy.

Constantine went beyond tolerance for the church, giving it legal freedom and equality. Bishops were given jurisdictional authority, as were civil magistrates. The clergy were not required to take part in civil duties, and Sunday was made a compulsory day of religious observance. In their prayers, soldiers were required to recognize Christian faith along with pagan rites. Constantine was caught up in various theological debates and, early in his rule, used the power of his office to decide on orthodoxy in the church. For example, he set up the Nicene Council to handle the controversy of Arianism, which stated that Jesus was not eternal but created. Although he gave the council freedom to debate, and even accepted the council's decision, which affirmed that Jesus was divine, it was evident that the hand of the emperor was now on the church.

He saw the state as responsible for regulating religion. Because the emperor had been responsible for overseeing pagan religions, it was a logical extension for him to also oversee Christianity. He was *ex officio* head of the church as well as head of state.

The rule of Constantine was such a sudden change from the old ways that the church had no time to formulate its views. Whereas the state and church had been very distinct, now there was a mingling of the two, to the extent that the state saw as its role the Christianizing of society. It was Constantine's son Constantius who went further and is reported to have said, "What I will, let that be reckoned as canon."[11] Tearing down the remains of paganism, he made himself appear a Christian emperor.

The relationship of the church and the civil order underwent an important shift when the church was called on to take a larger role in the administration of local government. The Roman Empire, going through an increased crisis of management as a result of such matters as crop failure and barbarian invasions, consolidated its power by centralizing and eliminating municipal self-government. Because bishops were elected by their communities and more citizens were turning to Christian faith, bishops were seen as leaders and people of influence, and were called on to judge disputes and care for widows and orphans. Gradually they came to take on local leadership in both religious and civil matters.

Constantine, in moving the centre of the Roman Empire to ancient Byzantium (later renamed Constantinople, then Istanbul), made himself head of the Christian church in the eastern section of the Empire. He built elaborate structures and surrounded himself with spectacular and ostentatious religious celebrations in which people would prostrate themselves before him. In his public appearances, he expected people to greet him with shouts of "Holy! Holy! Holy!" A new feature had been introduced, called "Caesaropapism": the emperor of Rome now had power over the church. In the western centre of Rome, though distant from the spectacular developments in the eastern centre of Constantinople, Roman popes increased splendor and pomp in their ceremonies, even as Constantine was doing in the east.

In the wide-ranging Roman Empire, with its fragmented moral life, the church provided moral guidelines in areas such as marriage and family. As the church increased its influence, the lives of the citizens were shaped by the doctrine and teaching of the church. In this way, the church had a salutary impact on society.

The Christendom Model

Once Constantine made Christianity the official religion, the Christian church began to greatly influence, if not rule, society. Though church leaders considered the church and state two separate kingdoms, the church increasingly played a strong role. Referred to as "Christendom," church authorities more and more influenced society as well as church matters.

The church and state over time became almost inseparable. The church's message was mixed with concerns of exercising power. Constantine, even if well intentioned, failed to see the need for distance between state and church. Assuming the two to be one, he gave social dignity to Christians who frequently had been maligned and harassed, even to death. By taking over as head of the church, he effectively ended martyrdom, but he also muddied the waters of spiritual purity by adding in social and cultural self-interest.

This church under Rome is too different and distant to be a model for today. As emperor, Constantine was so steeped in running the religious and ceremonial life that for him not to take Christianity and guide it was unthinkable. In the end, the small, suffering church was changed suddenly into a community of politically and socially empowered people. To be a Christian had now become an advantage. Along with this rise in status came a loss of focus and commitment. The refiner's fire burned low in lives that had been lived out of love and devotion to God, not social standing or political power.

The Holy Roman Empire

From AD 600 to 1000, a period known as "the Dark Ages," the western Roman Empire was assaulted by barbarians. In the early 800s,

Charlemagne, a pious and yet powerful warrior, ruled as emperor over much of the old Roman Empire. On Christmas day, 800, he was crowned by Pope Leo III as emperor. His son Louis went to Rome in 816 to receive the crown from the Pope, a public admission that political authority could be finally given only by the church. This submitting to the Pope was an open acknowledgment that the church was a higher power than the state.

Throughout the Middle Ages, the growth of the church and its increased hold on political life led to its dominating the state. But with its increased secular/political power, the church failed to provide effective spiritual leadership. Then, as the church lost its political hold, Christendom became more of a connection of various states. In 1302, Pope Boniface VIII was unequivocal about the absolute dominance of the papacy. In a quarrel with Philip of France, he wrote in the papal bull *Unam sanctam*: "It is altogether necessary to salvation for every human creature to be subject to the Roman pontiff."[12] However, the pontiff soon died; no ruler pursued this quarrel, and succeeding popes did not punish Philip. The monarchies had now gained too much power for Rome. However, it would be 200 years before the authority of Rome would crack from internal pressure.

THE REFORMATION

In the early 1600s, Christendom still ruled most of Europe. But within fifty years, that arrangement would change. The relationship of the church's power and the state's power was about to alter radically.

For centuries it had been assumed that the state and church were to be intertwined. Changing views on the relationship of the two did not—even in the sixteenth and seventeenth centuries—lead to the assumption that the spiritual had no place in the temporal. That debate came out of the European Enlightenment of the early 1800s. However, at this time (the early 1500s), it was quite unthinkable for the state to be independent from the church. A close union of secular and religious life was assumed to be fitting and theologically acceptable.

Three church leaders, offering different views of the relationship of the church and state, emerged in the early 1500s: Martin Luther, John Calvin, and Menno Simons.

The Luther Model

Martin Luther, a teacher of theology, set loose the Protestant Reformation in 1517 with his famous Ninety-Five Theses. He challenged papal authority, believing that faith alone, not the mediating work of the church, justifies. For him, redemptive faith was a gift of God; the church held a secondary role in salvation. The decrepit state of the Roman church only served to reinforce Luther's view that as a human instrument the church could be polluted. The final straw that broke his support of Rome was a scandal in which Pope Leo X allowed the buying of "indulgences" to help him pay for renovating St. Peter's in Rome. Tetzel, the German salesman of the indulgences, preached that a money payment would deliver a soul from purgatory. This proved to be too much for Luther.

As well, for Luther a group of Christians meeting together constituted a church. The priesthood was not a special or privileged body, independent of the Christian community. In his view, faith rooted in one's relationship to God kept one from undue concern with world-centred issues, and the church was not to see itself as a competitor of the state.

That is not to say that for Luther the state was not important. Indeed, it was. It had plenty to do: "The world and greater number of men are and always will be unchristian, even if they are all baptized and called Christians."[13] Given his view of the depravity of the human person, the state—as God's provision—was a force with a duty to perform. The primary role of the state was to repress wickedness and inflict punishment on the evildoer. He viewed the two kingdoms as necessary but always looked forward to the final triumph of the church in the world.

In *On Secular Authority, And How Far One Owes Obedience to It,* he wrote:

> Here we must divide the children of Adam and all men into two parts, the first belonging to the kingdom of God and the second to the kingdom of the world. Those who belong to the kingdom of God are all true believers in Christ, and are subject to Christ. For Christ is the King and Lord in the kingdom of God. ... The gospel should also be called a gospel of the kingdom of God, because it teaches, governs and maintains the kingdom of God. ...All who are not Christians belong to the kingdom of the world and are subject to the law.[14]

Although Luther divided the role of the two realms, as political and social disorder increased (tens of thousands of Anabaptists were killed by both Luther's followers and Catholics, and the Catholic resistance against the Protestant Reformation), he called on the state to re-establish order and rescue the church from what he saw as the tyranny of Rome, invoking the power of the prince to suppress Anabaptists and dissenting peasants. The irony is that in the end the church he initiated attached itself to the German state and, by so doing, became its subject.

The Calvin Model

Sixteenth-century reformer John Calvin was a remarkable thinker and leader. By age thirty, he had completed writing the massive *Institutes*, his biblical commentary. Eventually, Calvin moved to Geneva, where later he ruled unopposed as a dictator and instituted his vision of the church as the ruler of society.

Like Luther, Calvin challenged the Christendom model by asserting that the state received its authority from God directly, and not from the church. The state did not have unlimited authority; its power was circumscribed by the authority given it by God. However, that did not restrain the church from influencing the state. Indeed, the work of the church was to reform the state. Calvin even went so far as to contend that the state was to be used in Christianizing the world but not converting it, for conversion was the sole work of God in the individual.

He did differ with Luther's view of the restoration of the created order. For Calvin, the world was not to be left on its own; God's people were called to engage it in renewal. In his view, being a disciple meant going beyond the Lutheran understanding of inward salvation to the believer as part of God's plan to bring renovation to all the world by ruling it.

For Calvin, God's will was the source of all life, be it the church, the individual, or the state. His vision for the church was as a redeeming factor at work as God was renewing the creation. This church was to extend its sway over the whole social order. The ruling of Geneva expressed that understanding. He once described the work of the reform movement in Poland as an effort to "establish the heavenly reign of God upon earth." As the gospel worked its way out into the world, those social and political structures that opposed the reign of God would eventually be destroyed, until the whole world would come under the full and undisputed reign of Christ. Even though this reality was to be far in the future, that would not deter the people of God from pursuing God's reign as agents of Christ restoring the entire nations of the world to God's holy and final rule.

In the end, the influence of both Luther and Calvin linked the church and state, so much so that throughout the eighteenth century most Europeans who worshiped in a Protestant church did so in a church sanctioned by the state.

The "Otherworldly" Model

On the other side of the Reformed experiment was the Radical Reformation, or Anabaptists. Best known for one of its leaders, Menno Simons, the movement held a dualistic view of the world. Because the state was part of the world system, Anabaptists believed that Christians should separate themselves from it. Simons describes the two kingdoms:

> The Scriptures teach us that there are two opposing princes and two opposing kingdoms: the one is the prince of peace, and the other is the prince of strife. Each of these princes has his particular kingdom and as the prince is, so is also the kingdom. The prince of peace is Christ Jesus; His kingdom is the kingdom of peace....[15]

For Luther, the two kingdoms are interlinked in this age. For Simons, it was the opposite. He saw two distinct kingdoms, one ruled by God and the other by Satan. The separation was clear and absolute. The world is where the demonic rules, and it is nothing but a place of sin and corruption.

For Menno Simons, obedience to the state was conditional; obedience to God took precedence. The state had no final authority, and neither did the church have authority over the state. They were to remain separate.

John Calvin, Menno Simons, and Martin Luther were contemporaries. Coming out of a culture dominated by the church of Rome and its overwhelming power in ruling Europe, these three reformers sought a model they believed was faithful to the Scriptures and yet spoke in practical ways to their situations.

Today there is a variety of political theories rising out of these models. As we reflect on the Christendom, Lutheran, Calvinist, and Anabaptist models, the important question is, how are we to understand the relationship of Christ's kingdom to the surrounding social and political realities?

LESSONS FROM THE EARLY CHRISTIANS

A Vision for Final Reality

The early church was driven by the expectation of being united with Christ. John the Apostle writes,

> Now we are children of God, and what we will be has not yet been made known. But we know that when he appears, we shall be like him, for we shall see him as he is. Everyone who has this hope in him purifies himself... (1 John 3:2-3).

Two thousand years later, we know that such a moment of history has not come. Some Christians foolishly become so absorbed in predicting the future, examining dates, events, personalities, and national movements, that they discredit the central place which the hope of

Christ's return has in Christian living. But such abuse should not corrode or diminish our hope.

Why is the *eschaton*—the coming of Christ and the final triumph of his kingdom—so neglected? Christians trapped by comfort and ease aren't compelled to expect Christ's coming. The accommodation we have made with the gods of this age—materialism, scientism, and hedonism, just to note a few—camouflages the underlying imperative that regardless of our own personal comfort, the new creation must take over the evil of this current age. A hostile kingdom seems less threatening when we eat at its table. Those of us living in secure and materially satisfying circumstances are unwittingly caught by an underlying assumption that the final and triumphant reign of the King is no longer necessary. The heartbeat of the New Testament pulsates with the expectation of Jesus' coming: something that is lost in the clutter of today's material abundance.

The Work of the Kingdom

The early church keeps us from interpreting the kingdom as being primarily concerned with the redemption of social systems. "Behold I make all things new" (Rev. 21:5) does not contain the assumption that the transforming of social structures will usher in the kingdom. John's reference is to the new heavens and new Earth that Christ will order at the end of history. It's not that social systems that shape our lives do not matter to the gospel. But to confuse the redemption God expects of people with reforming systems is to misunderstand the nature of Christ's salvation.

This is not to underplay the impact redemption can have on social realities. Indeed, it can make a difference. Human and social relationships, structures, and systems can be deeply affected by the way in which Christian disciples work out the meaning of their salvation in Christ.

THE ROLES OF CHURCH AND STATE

The early church made it clear that government is not to do the work of the church. Paul notes that the government has its own work to do: it is to encourage social good and discourage social evil (Rom. 13:1–7). The call of the church is to serve Christ. The state, though it is Christ's creation and under his authority, is not designed to serve Christians any more than it is to serve those of other faiths. Living in a country with a Christian heritage, we too easily assume that our government is to be particularly supportive of the Christian church over other religious views. The New Testament gives no such indication.

That is not to say that Christians have no right or role in insisting that the government act in proper ways. Note Paul's sit-in (Acts 16): he would not move until the authorities came and apologized for what they had done. He insisted that the governing authorities act properly. He may have been making a point so that the church would be given fair treatment, reminding the state of its responsibility to properly treat the church and others. We do not know.

Nor do we ask the church to do the work of the government. The church has its own task: it calls into fellowship people who believe in Jesus Christ; in this community (body), members are nourished, discipled, and equipped to go back into the world as public evidence of God being at work in their lives. When the church tries to rule a nation, it is inevitably co-opted into using political power.

Judgment on All of Life

The early church also teaches us that the surrounding order is under God's judgment. Living in a nation in which Christians have had a profound influence on public institutions, we may be inclined to believe that what we have is good, and that a little tinkering will make it even better. Or that if we could just construct a new system, then surely the kingdom of Christ would be fulfilled. But all systems and organizations, be they religious or not, are under Christ's judgment. In his letter to the church at Rome, Paul analyzes our rejection of God's truth:

> The wrath of God is being revealed from heaven against all the godlessness and wickedness of men who suppress the truth by their wickedness (Rom. 1:18).

Christ's kingdom stands apart from all other kingdoms.

The Reality of Darkness

The corroding influence of our modern cultural and intellectual sophistication desensitizes the contemporary church to what the early church faced head on: spiritual warfare. Out of our growing understanding of human personality, evil is downplayed and made to appear as an influence or force. Jesus had a different analysis. He defined evil as a living reality coming from Satan. In this world, in which the forces of good and evil do battle, we know that simply improving social systems or developing innovative political enterprises is not enough to undo the impact of evil.

Paul understood this:

> For though we live in the world, we do not wage war as the world does. The weapons we fight with are not the weapons of the world. On the contrary, they have divine power to demolish strongholds. We demolish arguments and every pretension that sets itself up against the knowledge of God, and we take captive every thought to make it obedient to Christ (2 Cor. 10:3–6).

The early church also understood this.

The Test of Truth in Living

The early church also provided a model for living. It was not cowed by death. Today, too often it appears that the church cares more about its physical landscaping than the witness of truth. Such a church will not be drawn to the costly call of Christ and the kingdom. It is so easy for a church that desires respect from the world to avoid conflict. Cloaked in this self-interest, the church is weak and without power, quite unable to deal with the tough moral issues of our time.

A Stand for Truth

In this age of religious pluralism, syncretism—a merging of religious faiths so that none is viewed as being truer than another—

becomes the politically acceptable and preferred response. The early church thought otherwise. Peter declared, "Salvation is found in no one else, for there is no other name under heaven given to men by which we must be saved" (Acts 4:12). This leaves no room for arrogance—regardless of how it may appear to others—but affirms that Christ's kingdom is about Christ and none other.

The church in its early years had little to do with the prevalent political arrangements. For good reason: Christians were trapped by a system that allowed them no voice. At the launching of the church on the day of Pentecost, it was a fragile and, at times, harassed religious sect. After AD 70, it dispersed throughout the Roman Empire. The history given in Acts deals only with the first few years of the church, a time when Christians were concerned primarily with doctrine and survival. We look to them and learn from their experiences, insights, and response to God's direction. In the absence of specific directives on a particular subject, we are reminded that though this history is instructive, it does not spell out all that faith has to say about life around us. The underlying principles are set in place, but they are still to be applied in each time and culture.

It is good for us to be reminded that when the early church did respond to a particular issue, it did so because it thought and believed what it did was best. And the Bible is faithful and accurate in its recording. For example, Christians in Jerusalem sold their goods and lived in a communal economic relationship. Does that mean the church was right then, and does it mean we should use it as our model for today? Early Christians worked out of their understanding at that time, doing what they thought was appropriate and behaving according to what they believed was God's direction.

One could make the case that what they did was not necessarily appropriate. Paul later had to raise money to help Christians in Jerusalem. Could it be they bankrupted themselves by selling their capital items? Just because their experiences were faithfully recorded does not mean that what they did is always right for Christians today.

We applaud their courage and learn from their mistakes, but we do not translate their experiences into doctrine (unless there is an explicit directive). We examine and learn, but we do not canonize their actions.

Living in a radically different age, we seek the call to be disciples of Christ, be that in relation to the community of faith or to the surrounding culture. We take clues given by Christ, the early church, and the church throughout history and use them as a guide, as we seek to do that which is faithful to the gospel and, in Christian terms, shape our social and political life.

6

Is Pluralism
Just a Modern Babel?

For many Christians the problems of newly arrived religious faiths seem at times to take precedence over the expression of Christianity, but the essential challenge to Christians comes from a different source.

My experience with people from other faiths is that they don't want expressions of Christian faith to be lost in our culture. As one person said, the reason he came to Canada was because Christianity had created a framework of fairness and openness. His conclusion? Now that he was here, why would he want it to be less Christian? All religions share the desire for fair opportunities to live out their faith; even their differing goals do not usually explain the clashing of ideas.

The clash comes from another quarter: secularism. That is the challenge for Christians in this pluralistic world, and it is to gaining an understanding of pluralism that we now turn our attention.

✝

For some Christians, pluralism is a threat; for others, an opportunity. Some Christians alarmed by modern pluralism argue that because of the long history of Christianity in their particular country, they should have the right to insist that society continue to adhere to the biblical principles and values, especially since all indicators show that a very large percentage still consider themselves to be Christian.

As well, Christians threatened by plural diversity ask what coexistence has to do with Christ's command to make disciples of all people. Inherent in the life of Christian faith is this inextinguishable light that seeks to illuminate the world. Such energy is not easily co-opted, and it is never satisfied with merely getting along.

What adds to this threat is the use of pluralism by authorities or institutions to prevent Christian faith from exercising influence in public life. When Christianity becomes just one among many world religions, it is no longer able to command any special place in public life.

Yes, many of our countries are pluralistic societies. The important difference now is that the plurality—the many different voices—has increased, and the laws rule that a majority view is no longer assured of holding prime position. Political theorist Paul Marshall writes,

> Our challenge is how are we to live as Christians in this plural society? How do we live with our neighbours? How do we love our neighbours in the political realm? How do we live together justly with people of very different views?[1]

To make sense of this issue, it is helpful to look at the primary ways pluralism is used. Here I distinguish between two of those ways: religious pluralism and cultural pluralism.

Religious pluralism is a view which asserts that because many religions exist, no single faith (or world view) can be truer than the others. This is itself a belief system, because it is something people believe to be true. Cultural pluralism is an arrangement whereby people of differing beliefs, ways, and backgrounds choose to live together. This is not a belief system, but a social arrangement.[2]

RELIGIOUS PLURALISM

Since religious pluralism is an assertion that one truth claim of faith is no truer than another, under this belief system Jesus is seen as an important prophet, but no truer than another. Lesslie Newbigin, former bishop of the Church of South India, explains that under religious pluralism

> the differences between the religions are not a matter of truth
> and falsehood, but of different perceptions of the one truth;
> that to speak of religious beliefs as true or false is inadmissible.[3]

Such a system of faith rejects even the possibility of a claim to truth—that one can say that something is true. The most that religious pluralism can say about truth is that it is relative. The implication, as Christian ethicist Max Stackhouse describes it, is that

> no vision of God, humanity, or the world could be judged to
> be any more valid than any other view, and that what we have
> is some passing opinion or contextual eruption that has no
> claim on us and for which no warrants could be given.[4]

For a religious pluralist like theologian Ernst Troeltsch, there is no transcendent meaning in history; there is nothing above and over all, and nothing transcendent can or ever will intersect human life. For him, all religions or world views are human expressions, each of which may be unique, but none of which is truer than the others. In that sense, all truth claims are relative and there is no authoritative standpoint. The resulting assumption is that no faith can ever make such a claim. Those who do are labeled intellectually fascist.[5]

Author Allan Bloom, in analyzing the contemporary university scene, says,

> Openness—and the relativism that makes it the only plausible
> stance in the face of various claims to truth and various ways

of life and kinds of human beings—is the great insight of our times. The true believer is the real danger.[6]

Bloom, writing with tongue in cheek, says the tragedy is that people who are convinced that truth, as such, exists, are out of sync with prevailing thinking. The implication is that because of the many choices, one cannot assert that something therefore is true. Increased choices create not just more choices, but confusion. "If the typical condition of premodern man is one of religious certainty, it follows that of modern man is one of religious doubt."[7] This doubt, fueled by multiple choices, philosophical argumentation, the mix of cultures, opportunity for travel, and the width and speed of the information highway, creates a superabundance of choices and a data overload that convinces people that in light of all of these realities, it is quite impossible, and even irresponsible, for anyone to contend for a truth claim.

A follower of Jesus of Nazareth refutes such conclusions. The arrival of Christ's kingdom dealt a death blow to denials of ultimate truth. In the mix of Hellenistic religious, cultural, political, philosophical, and mystical ideas and movements, Jesus announced his rule with no fuzziness over an exclusive truth claim. Jesus offered what no sect, military leader, Mother Earth religion, or great mind could: a way to understand all of life.

It was in those early days that the delusion of religious pluralism found its match.

In a fearful and capricious world, the gospel promised universal salvation in Jesus Christ; amidst cults of secrecy, the gospel was proclaimed openly in synagogues and market places; in a world searching for individual escape, the gospel took on the form of an organized church, a witnessing and sometimes suffering community of faith; and in an age when no way or truth was deemed compelling enough to demand the whole of human life, followers of Jesus Christ bore witness to their faith by the supreme sacrifice of martyrdom.[8]

Defending one's faith to the extent of martyrdom does not come from believing that all paths lead to the same gate. To respect the right of others to believe as they choose is one thing, but to believe that your faith is not qualitatively different from another, and then to die for your faith, is ludicrous. A professed Marxist, Professor Milan Machovec, commented, "I do not trust a Christian who isn't interested in converting me."[9] He understood Christian faith. He knew that at the heart of the gospel is a voice that calls us away from all other voices. Truth compels us to tell others because it is restless until others know of it.

As well, the logic of religious pluralism in alleging that all truth claims are equally true breaks down. For if each faith is said to be as valid as the others, it is called on to deny its own claim to truth.

Religious pluralism also confuses the very discussion of truth itself. Newbigin observes that the story of blindfolded people describing an elephant, often used to argue for religious pluralism, misses the point. One blindfolded person holding onto a leg describes the animal as a tree. Another, feeling the trunk, is sure it is the end of a fire hose. Each is convinced he has the truth. The conclusion? Nothing is really true; truth is only what one thinks is true, and each perception is equally valid.

The telling point of the story, however, is that as the blindfolded people fumble about in the dark, trying to decipher what they are touching, there is one person not blindfolded who knows the full truth about the animal. The sum total of life is not blindfolded people recounting their life experiences.

As a missionary in southern India, Newbigin observed that as he watched the acceptance of Jesus into the Hindu world, he, Newbigin, was seduced.

> Jesus had become just one figure in the endless cycle of *karma* and *samsara*, the wheel of being. ... He had been domesticated into the Hindu world view.[10]

It was over time that Newbigin recognized that by wanting a "reasonable Christianity," he had sought instead to explain the gospel in his own terms. He concludes, "I, too, had been guilty of domesticating the gospel." It is seductive to seek accommodation in order to avoid being seen as belligerent or insensitive. As well intentioned as this concern may be, it can lead to a modification of the message, a public posture of mutual acceptance, and the adoption of a world view of religious pluralism. Newbigin sounds a clear warning:

> As long as the Church is content to offer its beliefs modestly as simply one of the many brands available in the ideological supermarket, no offense is taken. But the affirmation that the truth revealed in the gospel ought to govern public life is offensive.[11]

Religious pluralism is an easy way out. It blurs the Christian affirmation of Jesus: "I am the way and the truth and the life. No one comes to the Father except through me" (John 14:6). Jesus' words are tough and exclusive. But to skip over his assertion is to miss the point of his coming.

CULTURAL PLURALISM

At its centre, religious pluralism maintains that truth is relative. In the end, it is a belief system. Cultural pluralism is very different. It is not a belief system but rather a means of coexisting without resorting to legislative or physical war. It is an attitude that allows the constructing of social harmony, believing that people of differing ideologies, faith, cultures, and living standards can actually coexist. It does not mean that one group must give up their right to believe or assert that their faith is truth. In places such as Northern Ireland and Bosnia, sites of conflict between different religions or outright warfare or oppression by the ruling religion, cultural pluralism does not operate. Social commentator Don Posterski says that "a culture that is both 'principled' and 'pluralistic' invites people to be true to themselves, but also makes room for diversity."[12]

Religious pluralism is an enemy, whereas cultural pluralism is an opportunity. Western countries are composed of many cultures. This was true from our very beginnings. For example, in my father's Swedish community, assemble a hundred Swedes and you would find a mixture of liberals and conservatives, socialists, and free-market advocates. This is cultural pluralism—various ideas, religions, and values living with respect for each other, though at times in sharp disagreement.

Today most Western nations have an increasingly mixed national heritage, no longer made up primarily of aboriginal and European communities. Wars, famines, dictators, disease, education, and commerce have driven people from their native countries and, in their search for a homeland, increased the cultural mix and diversity. It is in this world of cultural pluralism that the kingdom lives and Christ's people are called to live, minister, and affect all of life.

Newbigin defines cultural pluralism as an "attitude which welcomes the variety of different cultures and lifestyles within one society and believes that this is an enrichment of human life." He goes on to say that though he accepts cultural pluralism, he wants to "qualify that acceptance with the obvious point that cultures are not morally neutral. There are good and bad elements in culture."[13] This point is critical, for if we fall into the trap of approving of other cultures out of our attempt to be cordial, we end up blind to moral flaws that are injurious to us all.

Cultural pluralism is a simple recognition of the many. It is not an affirmation of all aspects of culture, nor that cultures are the same. It is a descriptive label. It recognizes that cultures and faiths (or world views) exist and that they have a right to exist. For example, I disagree with homosexuals on their view of what is biblically normative. I also disagree with many of their public policies. But I accept that they exist as members of this society and they have a right to represent their concerns, to vote, to be employed, and to receive the same protection as all citizens.

Cultural pluralism, though, is not just an idea picked up as a social theory to help us all get along. It is a basic Christian affirmation that we—as God does—are to give space and allowance for people to think, believe, act, and hope with different assumptions. It is Jesus, with the unexpected directive to love others ("Love your enemies and pray for those who hurt you," Matt. 5:44), who revolutionizes our way of treating others, including those who believe and act differently.

The apostle Paul, in counseling Christians in Rome on how to live with others, built on Jesus' words:

> Live in harmony with one another. Do not be proud, but be willing to associate with people of low position. Do not be conceited. Do not repay anyone evil for evil. Be careful to do what

is right in the eyes of everybody. If it is possible, as far as it depends on you, live at peace with everyone (Rom. 12:14–18).

Before the fourth century, Christians in Rome were a despised minority, living out a faith new to the broader culture. They had no privileged position. Indeed, they were persecuted and martyred. It is helpful to ask what life would be like in a country where Christian faith had no historical precedence or favored position. If Christians in Rome were called to live in peace with others when they were a very small minority without any historically favored position, how much more should that message be heard by Christians who live with the benefits of democracy and human rights?

The writer of Hebrews calls for Christians to "make every effort to live in peace with all men and to be holy" (Heb. 12:14); Peter says, "Show proper respect to everyone: Love the brotherhood of believers, fear God, honour the king" (1 Peter 2:17); Jesus, in the Sermon on the Mount, reminds us that goodness is extended to all: "He causes his sun to rise on the evil and the good, and sends rain on the righteous and the unrighteous." Jesus challenges their attitude toward those outside of their circle of faith: "And if you greet only your brothers, what are you doing more than others? Do not even pagans do that?" (Matt. 5:47).

The Scriptures leave no room for an end run. We are mandated to live at peace. No questions asked! Church of England pastor and teacher John Stott explains that

> in social action...we should neither try to impose Christian standards by force on an unwilling public, nor remain silent and inactive before the contemporary landslide, nor rely exclusively on the dogmatic assertion of biblical values, but rather reason with people about the benefits of Christian morality, commending God's law to them by rational arguments. We believe that God's laws are both good in themselves and universal in their application because, far from being arbitrary, they fit the human beings God has made.[14]

This understanding frees us from assuming that having the church at the centre of political power is the same thing as doing the work of

the King. Often in countries where Christian faith is culturally dominant, while Christians are assured of a place in the political hierarchy,
the church loses its spiritual edge. Lost is the need for people to live the
Christlike life of suffering, holiness and love. The church, calloused by
prestige and power, loses sight of the persistent reminder to make disciples. There is a purifying process in having to live out Christ's claims
in an unbelieving world. Testing Christ's call in a hostile world has its
own rewards. As Newbigin says, "Religious experience occurs in the
sanctuary, but its claim to truth has to be tested in the public
world..."[15] Truth obliged is offensive, but truth defended is life.

IMPLICATIONS OF CULTURAL PLURALISM

Cultural pluralism is different from religious pluralism in that it is
not a faith system. Cultural pluralism recognizes the importance of
public justice for all, without discrimination because of religion. That is
why the affirmation of cultural pluralism is so important. It is unfortunate that too often Christians are spooked by the word "pluralism,"
assuming that what is meant is syncretism. To build up cultural pluralism is to build up freedoms which, in turn, allow Christians to live
more freely and witness of their faith. In countries where there is individual freedom, a high school student can know that even if his or her
faith is opposed by others in the class, he or she is assured of having the
right to talk about it in school. The importance of understanding cultural pluralism is made clear by this very point. If the student is marginalized in the class or given a lower grade because his or her view does
not align with that of the teacher, the teacher should be challenged.
Cultural pluralism is a very strong defense against any ideological
tyranny that might attempt to rule in our public schools and universities. It does not mean a loss of freedom, for Christians or for people of
any other faith. It does mean that if a church enjoyed special privileges
because of its size or access to power in the past, it no longer does.

It is true that sometimes in public life cultural pluralism is used
to prohibit Christians from having a voice. For example, in Canada in
recent years, some municipalities disallowed nativity scenes, and some
school districts eliminated any mention of Jesus Christ—even

Christmas trees—at Christmas. This is an exploitation of cultural pluralism. Instead, each faith represented in that community should have
the right to show its symbols at special times of the year. The mistake
is to assume that cultural pluralism eliminates expression. Political
theorist Paul Marshall compares it to students gathering on the play-
ground. The teacher asks what the children want to play. Someone
calls out "baseball," another "skipping," another "football," and
another, "I don't want to play." "Well," the teacher responds, "since
we cannot agree, we won't play at all." Cultural pluralism offers the
opposite view: each person should have the right to public expression.

As well, cultural pluralism is not designed to thwart the ability of
people to influence our society. Though the Christian faith is no longer
accorded special status, cultural pluralism does provide the framework
in which people and groups are able to put forward their concerns and
ideas. It then becomes a forum of open debate, not a muzzle.

The problem for some Christians is that they assume that by
acknowledging pluralism they are trapped by compromise. I believe
the opposite. When, for example, a Christian argues against the wide-
spread practice of abortion, compromise occurs when, for the sake of
getting along, the other person responds, "I'll modify my belief so we
can get along." This is the opposite of working cultural pluralism.
Pluralism does not require people to change their views just to get
along. Instead, we hold firmly to our commitments and learn to work
with others, even though our views may be deeply divergent. Amid
the differences, we seek a way for coexistence, with neither side giving
up what it believes to be true.

For Christians who have known the central place of Christian
faith in their culture, cultural pluralism is a shocking new reality. The
religious majority no longer has preferred status, privilege, or the right
to rule. Christians in some countries think this loss of a preferred
position means they now hold fewer rights than do minorities. But if
an imbalance of rights does occur, it calls for a response. When people are given preferential treatment because of being in the majority
or minority—unless both sides agree that for particular reasons that is
good for a time—that treatment must be challenged.

In my country today, even while a large percentage call themselves

Christian, faith has little place in public debate. Christians need to challenge this. Cultural pluralism offers the right for people of faith to insist that media, governments, and school boards take seriously the right of people of faith to exercise their option to be at the table. Too often such opportunity is not allowed.

The tragedy is that the church has caved in to the privatizing of faith and has left society to run as it chooses. But for Christians serious about having an impact on our nation, cultural pluralism opens the door to influencing public life.

After a presentation to a federal parliamentary subcommittee one MP said, "Yes, but are not you trying to get us to accept a religious opinion? After all, this is a pluralistic world." He was right in what he said, but wrong in what that implied. Yes, I was expressing a definite Christian view. And yes, this is a pluralistic society. But he was wrong in his implied conclusion that because it was a Christian view, it was therefore not legitimate. Our country offers people an opportunity to express views and make choices. When this is not allowed to happen, Christians need to contest the unfairness, not just for themselves but for others.

Cultural pluralism is a way of living with mutual respect, yet without basic compromise. Immigrants who come from lands where religious intolerance is the rule recognize that Canada is built on the Christian view of the significance of the person and the right of people to make most choices without coercion. For Christians, especially those from a European or American background, this is an opportunity to unlink Christian faith from position and history as a means of imposing Christ's ministry on society. My hope is that Christians will move beyond racial biases or favoritism, ensuring that others also have a country to call their own.

THE WEAKNESSES OF CULTURAL PLURALISM

Any social arrangement for living together has its weaknesses: it may result in some believing what Newbigin warns us against—that cultures are morally neutral. No culture is free of self-interests or destructive habits. Note the shameful treatment historically in so many countries of aboriginal peoples. As wrong as that has been, it is also wrong to assume that their cultures are ideal. All cultures have flawed values and unacceptable behaviour, including attitudes—for example, of the Japanese toward the Koreans; Germans toward the Jews; and South African whites toward blacks. All of these attitudes rise out of cultures, none of which is morally neutral.

Another frailty of cultural pluralism is the effort to connect religious, cultural, and racial issues. It has been argued that cultural pluralism does not allow critique of a faith or culture, especially if the two are linked by way of racial origin.

In public there is often a bias against Christian faith. The educational debate of evolution versus creation is a clear example. Evolution—a theory that says the strong survive over the weak, and that humanity rose out of an undefined past—advocates a world view which holds no promise except the continual outworking of the principle of evolution. The biblical story of creation, on the other hand, is set within an understanding of the source of life, the struggle of humankind, and the hope of Christ and the kingdom.

Lesslie Newbigin says,

> These are two different and incompatible stories. One is taught as fact; the other—if it is taught at all—is taught as a symbolic way of expressing certain values in which some people, but not all, believe. The first is taught as what we know; the second as what some people think.[16]

Public schools tend to avoid the Bible story on the basis that it will violate the rights of those who hold other religious views. Actually the world view or belief system called "materialistic evolution" has been allowed to stand as the "factual" rendering of the beginnings of human life (though there is certainly scientific doubt as to the veracity of the evolution theory), which violates the rights of other religious views.

PLURALISM AS AN OPPORTUNITY

My wife, Lily, and I, along with a few friends, were traveling in Jerusalem. Peter, our Israeli driver and guide, turned a corner into a narrow lane at the same time another driver entered from the opposite direction. There they sat, front bumpers almost touching, eyes glaring, voices raised. Then fists flailed the air. Someone had to move. But for both drivers, to give in was the worst of possible options. We sat there until Peter, muttering and shaking his head at such humiliation, moved. We cheered him. We told him he was the winner because of his willingness to get along. I am not sure if he believed us, but at least he appreciated our applause.

Learning to live in cultural pluralism calls us to learn to work with those with whom we are in conflict. By so doing, we work out how we can live in the same community without "going for each other's throats." An example of this is the Second World War story of Corrie Ten Boom from Haarlem in the Netherlands. The Nazis had invaded Holland, capturing Jews and any who would attempt to save them. Corrie tells of the time when a pastor refused to help a Jewish couple who needed someone to care for their child. "No. Definitely not," the pastor said. "We could lose our lives for that Jewish child." Corrie's father stepped forward and, taking the baby up in his arms, was heard to say, "You say we could lose our lives for this child? I would consider that the greatest honour that could come to my family."[17] In a world in which Christian faith was dominant, the oppressed minority was seen as worth saving, even if it meant the Ten Boom family might become victims.

Cultural pluralism, for a Christian, is not just coexistence or civility. It is a way of working out the kingdom in real life. At the heart of living out Christ's kingdom is a desire to be a faithful witness to the evangel of Jesus, the good news that Jesus has come. With the realization of Jesus' coming, we see all of life differently. Cultural pluralism is not something to fear; though there are dangers, there are also enormous opportunities. True, wherever one lives, in whatever culture, there are always opportunities for evangelism. But a culture that affirms the pluralistic ideal offers an opportunity for Christian interaction and influence which is missing in single-religion cultures.

OCCUPYING

Jesus tells a story (Luke 19:11–27, KJV) about caring for investments. The words he used were "occupy until I return." This stands in contradistinction to a withdrawing. In telling this story of a man of noble birth, Jesus makes it clear that the workers were to be diligent in managing investments entrusted to them by their master. They were to manage in such a way that on his return, those investments would have appreciated. He further reinforces the enormous responsibility each servant has in caring for what has been trusted to him. On his return, the master queries each on how well he has done. The first two are praised for their success. The third—who hid his talents in fear of the master—is handed out a most devastating judgment: "Take and throw him into hell fire." The tough consequences for disobedience meted out to the third servant are not a punishment for evil, but rather for failing to do what was requested.

To "occupy" in a culture of pluralism does not mean to just seek peace and harmony at the expense of truth-telling. Our calling is not to line up, as Lesslie Newbigin says, as if we are making contributions to a pot-luck supper. At the heart of our calling is a truth question which insists on a truth answer.

In Nazi Germany, a small group of Christian leaders found that their contribution to the debate on Jewry and nationalism was not enough. Led by German theologian and pastor Dietrich Bonhoeffer, they decided to reject the accommodation to the Nazis that some of their church colleagues had made. Some years later, at dawn on April 9, 1945, his young life was cut short by a Nazi hangman. He had risen up against the evils of Nazism and spoken in uncompromising terms, and for that his life was lost while others of his colleagues were drowned in a sea of compromise to the powerful Nazi machine.

Early in his life, Dietrich Bonhoeffer was interested in theology and faith. Beginning as a professor, he eventually saw his true calling to be a pastor. But a quiet pastoral life was not to be his. In a country caught up in the racist nationalism of Hitler, Bonhoeffer was called on to take a stand and to discern the evil of this rising empire within his own fatherland. He chose to voice strong opposition during a time in which most church leaders were knuckling under to the wishes of the Führer.

His concerns led him to join up with the Confessing Church, founded in 1933 by Pastor Martin Niemöller. Under the influence of

Karl Barth, they wrote and signed the famous Barmen Declaration, which laid the basis for the resistance against the Nazis' attempt to make the Evangelical Churches an instrument of Nazi policy. In this document they outlined their deep opposition to extreme nationalism and the subverting of the gospel of Christ to political power. Bonhoeffer eventually was forbidden by the Nazis to preach, and was removed from his teaching post.

When the war broke out, he was in America on a preaching tour. He knew what faced him if he returned, but he believed God was calling him back. He could not imagine staying away from his Christian colleagues when they were undergoing such oppression.

He did return, and in 1943 was arrested and imprisoned by the Gestapo at Flossenbürg. In 1945 he was hanged, but he left a legacy to all Christians, calling on us to occupy, even when deep personal sacrifice is required. His most powerful writings are contained in his book *The Cost of Discipleship*, much of which was written while he was in prison. I recall that in university his words caught my attention: when God calls you, he calls you to die.

The heartbeat of Christian service is to live one's life for truth. This is done within the framework of the one we serve: Jesus Christ. He made himself of no reputation, but became obedient, not to the power structures of Rome, but to the humiliating and deadening effect of the cross. The spirit that needs to cloak us as we work out our salvation and articulate a biblical vision of life "is not an imperial power, but the slain lamb."[18]

7

Speaking a New Language

This final chapter is as close as I get to noting specific actions we can take. You'll have seen that my interest is in what it means to be disciples of Christ in a world where the public sphere is often hostile to spiritual insights and understanding.

My vision is of Christians active in the public square. But what should be the nature of that action? How do I, as a citizen of my country and a disciple of Christ, engage in public life?

As much as I love my country, there is need here for a new vision. That vision will come only as people filled with Christ's life speak a language of public discourse with truth and love.

May these final thoughts give hope for what Christ can do in our personal lives and in our nations. It is, after all, only by his empowerment that we can live out the kingdom within the social and political framework of the land in which we live.

✝

WHAT IS TO BE OUR ATTITUDE?

In looking from Babel to Calvary, we've asked what a biblically informed nation looks like. Even deeper is the question of what Christians have to bring to enhance the qualities of their country.

Christians who long for a more Christian country and insist on biblical principles as a right misunderstand Christ's kingdom. For 2,000 years Christians have struggled with finding the right relationship of faith to country. H. Richard Niebuhr, in *Christ and Culture*, suggests that Christians' attempts, in various times and circumstances, to meld their commitment to Christ with the political order can be described in five ways: Christ against culture, Christ of culture, Christ above culture, Christ and culture in paradox, and Christ the transformer of culture.[1]

I find Niebuhr's approaches helpful, but not one is right for all times. Yes, the kingdom has a transformative effect on society as "salt" and "light." Contemporary political events suggest it is so.

The revolution in Romania, which ended the oppressive Ceauşecu regime in the late 1980s, is an example of such transformative effects. One night, not long before this vicious government fell, Ceauşecu ordered soldiers to move in on a crowd protesting the regime. The people, carrying lighted candles, surrounded the church in the square to protect their pastor, who, as leader of the revolt, was hiding in the church. The next day, as the pastor was visiting the wounded in hospital, he met a young man whose leg had been mutilated by a bullet. After some words of encouragement, the man looked up at the pastor and said, "Don't feel sorry for me. You see, my candle was the first to be lit. Everyone got the flame from me. The price of my leg was worth it." This young man, along with thousands of others, faced a treacherous and violent government. By his faith and courage, the minister was a transforming influence in that country.

In South Africa in 1994, tension was running high as the spring election approached—the first in which blacks would have full democratic franchise. However, there was a rift between two major black factions. If the Inkatha Freedom Party, led by Zulu Mangosuthu Buthelezi, continued to refuse to participate in the election, blood might be shed among black factions. Professor Washington Okumu, a mediator with the Organization of African Unity from Kenya and a practising Christian, was asked to assist in bringing about an agreement between Buthelezi and Nelson Mandela, head of the African National Party.

Michael Cassidy, of African Enterprise, had worked for years to bring about reconciliation among the races. He was present on April 15 when Okumu and Buthelezi were to meet at the Johannesburg airport. Okumu was late for the appointment, and so Buthelezi left to fly home, even though Cassidy tried to persuade him to wait. All Cassidy could do was pray. Buthelezi's plane taxied for take-off, but a malfunction forced it to return to the terminal. By then Okumu had arrived, and the meeting took place. Over time the Inkatha Party agreed to participate in the elections, undoubtedly saving countless lives. Without political office, Cassidy exercised political influence by building relationships and supporting leaders through encouragement and prayer. The *Durban Daily News* carried the headline "How God stepped in to save South Africa." They quoted Buthelezi:

> It was [as] though God had prevented me from leaving [the airport] and I was there like Jonah, brought back. ...My forced return was a God-send.

The church is part of a bipolarity: it stands against world-centred ideologies. Christians have a reforming presence by opposing powers that run contrary to biblical values. Here are five different ways Christians relate to the public order: through personal involvement, through institutional engagement, as the alternative community, as the "arm's-length" community, and through withdrawal.

Personal Involvement

This view is that the mission of each Christian is to engage personally in public life: because this is God's world, we are called to engage. There is an awakening among Christians to the critical importance that decisions on public policy have for us all. To ignore them is to jeopardize our future and the well-being of one's nation.

For some years I served in my country as a national spokesperson for evangelicals, who constitute more than ten per cent of the population. There has been a remarkable rise of interest in public-policy issues and an increased personal commitment to take action. This commitment makes itself known on issues such as abortion, euthanasia, violence in the home and in the media, attempts to redefine marriage, and the role of parents in education. These issues have galvanized people into forming groups and associations in local, provincial, and national communities.

From an urgent sense of needing to "do something about it," Christians from both Protestant and Catholic faiths have run for office at provincial and federal levels, as well as at the local level of school boards. At an even more grass-roots level—by attending meetings, writing letters, and raising money—the Christian electorate has expressed this profound desire to make a difference.

This application of what I believe Christ is calling us to by way of public leadership and engagement rises out of my own experience. I make no pretense that this will work for all. I have been with too many of my brothers and sisters who struggle with dictatorship, religious intolerance, and police control not to realize the many and varied situations in which Christians live.

This outline is an attempt to give you a framework for engagement which takes into account the call of Christ to live with his power and truth and not be bound by the world-driven concern over power.

Institutional Engagement

This comes from the belief that institutions and organizations are the most effective forum for dealing with issues of public concern. New organizations—including new political movements—often rise out of this view. Problems are seen as being more societal than individual. In various parts of the world, the Social Gospel movement of the early twentieth century symbolizes this approach.

Once the shift was made from the historic view that sin was personal to the perception that sin is social, institutions became the primary issues of concern. Christians shaped by this understanding formed protest groups, which led to political action and organization.

The Alternative Community

This view asserts that Christians are called to transform culture. Christian Reformed communities (many with a Dutch origin) build alternative structures in politics, education and labour. They set up Christian organizations shaped by their theological tradition in order to influence the mainstream.

For example, they pioneered the Christian school movement. Even at great personal cost—having to pay tuition for their children as well as public-school taxes—the majority of them send their children to private Christian schools at the primary, secondary and university levels.

The Arm's-length Community

Not to be confused with the withdrawal approach, an arm's-length approach seeks to build a church community that is distinct from the world. The purpose is not only to avoid worldly enterprise, but to model a very different community. Anabaptists (better known as Mennonites) have provided us with this model.

This is different from the alternative-organization model in that the goal is to be faithful to the gospel on a community level, rather than to transform culture. The fear inherent in this model is that by engaging the ruling powers, there is a temptation to use the same levers of influence as those who make no confession of kingdom faith. Adherents of the arm's-length approach believe that Christians are to live for Christ without resorting to political power. Yet, at the same time, by setting up a purer biblical and Christlike model, they will be able to influence the wider culture. John Howard Yoder was a political writer in the Mennonite community. He put it this way:

The key to the ultimate relevance and to the triumph of the good is not any calculation at all, paradoxical or otherwise, of efficacy, but rather simple obedience. Obedience means not keeping verbally enshrined rules but reflecting the character of the love of God. The cross is not a recipe for resurrection. Suffering is not a tool to make people come around, nor a good in itself. But the kind of faithfulness that is willing to accept evident defeat rather than complicity with evil is, by virtue of its conformity with what happens to God when he works among men, aligned with the ultimate triumph of the Lamb.[2]

Withdrawal

This was very much the guiding view of many evangelicals during the early and mid-twentieth century. This view was fueled by a heightened expectation that because the return of Christ was seen to be imminent, the only right way to serve Christ was to have as little to do with the systems of the world as possible, and instead get ready for eternity. Some even refused to allow their members to vote.

Within each of the above approaches there is a wide continuum. The withdrawal view, for example, includes a curious assortment: on one side there is the Amish community, who choose to live alone on their own farming settlements; on the other side is my own Pentecostal tradition. Up to the late 1950s, although part of the social mainstream, Pentecostals interpreted the Bible's call as requiring a withdrawal from social and political life. It was assumed that with the Lord's return just around the corner—and God's obvious lack of interest in an impermanent world—we were to live apart. This is an example of recent shifts within many Christian groupings in moving from the social fringe to a more aggressive stance in taking their place at the table of social concern.

Which approach to Christian living is most biblical? Each has a legitimate case to make, depending on times and circumstance. Indeed, each approach can seem to be appropriate at different times. The problem is that responses tend to be institutionalized and take on bureaucratic structures, becoming entrenched in church life.

Working out of these models developed through the centuries, each generation must decide which approach or synthesis is appropriate, based on what they understand of the call of Christ, the needs of society, and the political and social structures of the time. That said, an increasing number of Christians agree that the Scriptures and the Spirit are calling Christians to engage and participate in public discourse and leadership. The well-being of each of our countries depends on Christians who will engage in public leadership so that biblical values of truth, integrity and justice pervade the legislative agenda. We should not be duped into believing that such engagement will completely reform our land. Nor should we see it as a mandate to reimpose the Christendom model. Rather, it is a call to live out the gospel in a redemptive way, with an eye to Jesus' return and with a heart of obedience.

Not to take hold of the many tough and challenging issues our nation faces is to fail both Christ's call and our country.

THE TASK OF A NATION

Paul notes that the task of the political state and public servants is to serve: "For he [the ruler] is God's servant to do you good" (Rom. 13:4).

So what do we do with the growing resentment against the high cost of government? While government must always be carefully critiqued, the Bible views public employees as servants. At the same time, government employees need reminding of what such a calling requires of them. For Christians living in a democracy, here is what we can expect from our nation.

To Organize

People need organization, whether they live in the wilderness or in congested urban sprawl. People thrown together in refugee camps or prisons end up organizing themselves into working groups. No one tells them they must; they just do. Moses learned that the only way he could function was to divide the people into groups and appoint leadership. You cannot get food, arrange for accommodation, resolve disputes, and care for sanitation without organization. For people to fulfill God's will, a place of relative calm is required. Nations have the structures to provide that. (That is not to say that Christians living in less favorable situations aren't effective in working out their Christian commitment.)

Organization implies agreed-upon rules. People need to understand the common ground in the group. The development of rules happens through the struggles and interplay of the community; they arise democratically through process or are imposed by a ruling body or person.

The strength of a nation is its people, and the strength of a people grows as they are encouraged to use their gifts. An organized community, by a responsible and fair division of labour, builds up the strength of the nation. As well, people are given freedom to work in an environment without fear that they will be overtaken by an enemy, by anarchy, or by fellow citizens who violate societal rules.

To Protect

Members of the Hebrew nation expected their king to protect them from foreign enemies. Guards were constantly on the alert in case of attack. Such protective measures were essential to the survival of the nation during its wanderings and once it was established in Canaan.

An unprotected people, caught up in the struggle for survival, lack the freedom to progress. An unprotected society is fearful and unproductive. The crucible in which life issues are tested needs to be secure. A good nation then becomes the place in which people are allowed to live out the purposes of God.

We agree that the government's role is to protect and administer justice, but a caution is appropriate. To simply remind government of its task and then to walk away is to misunderstand the nature and call of government as only one factor in the Christian life. If there is one mission field calling for kingdom ingenuity and presence, it is the field of justice and criminal reform. The hearts of criminals, often battered and abused in childhood, need spiritual reconstruction. Correction and rehabilitation ought to be at the heart of our mandate: the insight and power of Christian faith ought to be a force acting against the tragic realities of crime and abuse.

To Care for Its People

One cannot read Old Testament prophets and not be impressed with their focus on the needs of the fatherless, widows, refugees, the physically violated, the hurting, the sick and the impoverished. They reminded the nation that God judged not on political arrangements or military might, but on how the people treated the needy, marginalized and hurting.

The people of Israel, including some landowners who were exploiting their workers while professing their own piety, had so distorted the meaning of religious fasting that Isaiah rebuked them strongly, then offered this definition of a true fast:

> Is not this the kind of fasting I have chosen: to loose the chains of injustice and untie the cords of the yoke, to set the oppressed free and break every yoke? Is it not to share your food with the hungry and to provide the poor wanderer with shelter—when you see the naked, to clothe him, and not to turn away from your own flesh and blood? (Isa. 58:6, 7).

Prior to the modern state, many of our charitable efforts were made at the instigation of the church. Today, the complexity of life, the diminishing role of the church, and the growing role of state reinforce our interdependence. How we care for our citizens in need is a measurement of the quality of our nation. This is not to give *carte blanche* approval to all government bureaucracies, nor is it to say that government departments are the most effective means of serving people's needs. A legitimate concern is that the charitable nature of a country's social safety net may be exploited and, in the end, create a preference in some of its users for social support over work. Yet, a fundamental task of the state is to care for those most adversely affected by poverty and injustice.

To Be a Model of Justice and Mercy

Policies and legislation of a government not only resolve issues, but serve to signal to the society what it believes is best. Some assume that government doesn't legislate morality. But the truth is that each government bill, whether on abortion, taxation, or money, is a legislation imposing a moral view of life. Morality—defined as what a people believe is right—is always at stake in rules that define how people ought to act. While spirituality cannot be legislated, governments do set moral guidelines, whether they know it or not.

Too often people with deeply held religious convictions want governments to legislate laws supportive of their own views. The call to government is to be just—that is, to be fair and not to implement legislation that favors one group over another. For a government to force people to live by the beliefs of any religion would be unjust, even if the citizens accept these beliefs as basic for national life. There is no biblical mandate that suggests government should enforce any religious beliefs. The government is not called on to do the work of the church. Jesus did not call the government to go into all the world and preach the gospel. The requirement of government is to support a fair and just environment so its citizens can live in an orderly, peaceful way, free from an arbitrary imposition of values and beliefs.

Justice also includes respect for ethnic diversity. Racial animosity is fuel to many wars. A lack of respect for other races is often a manifestation of fear or arrogance. A nation's multiracial strains can, in moments of national disunity, become targets of abuse. With countries increasingly being mixed by immigrants it becomes complex. And in this setting, is there a Christian response? Yes, there is. With Christ as Creator, all of humanity is God's expression. While cultures will clash, our witness of Christ is measured by how we speak and treat others. Christians are called to live so that our witness expresses Christ's rule.

To Choose Its Political System

Reinhold Niebuhr commented that democracy is that child of which Christianity need never be ashamed. Even so, there is no single biblical political system. Neither democracy nor any other political formula is noted in the Bible as an appropriate political model.

Countries with a Christian heritage have been blessed because their political ideals, and even their political parties, have been influenced by Christian thought and leaders. A former prime minister, Pierre Elliott Trudeau, reminded fellow citizens that

> the golden thread of faith is woven throughout the history of Canada from its earliest beginnings up to the present time. Faith was more important than commerce in the minds of many of the European explorers and settlers, and over the centuries, as successive waves of people came to this country, many in search of religious liberty, they brought with them a great wealth and variety of religious traditions and values. Those values have shaped our laws and our lives, and have added enormous strength to the foundation of freedom and justice upon which this country was built. ...It was in acknowledgment of that debt that the Parliament of Canada later gave its approval during the Constitutional debate to the statement that Canada is founded upon principles that recognize the supremacy of God and the rule of law. Faith played a large part in the lives of so many men and women who have created in this land a society which places a high value on commitment, integrity, generosity and, above all, freedom. To pass on that heritage strong and intact is a challenge worthy of all of us who are privileged to call ourselves Canadians.

To that the Rt. Hon. Joe Clark, another former prime minister, added:

> I ask that we never forget the faith and the vision of the people who originally brought this country together, the Fathers of Confederation, who from the depths of their own profound faith took as their guide a verse from the Psalms of David, the verse that has since become the motto for our nation: "He shall have dominion also from sea to sea, and from the rivers to the ends of the earth." We pray that God's sovereignty over our Canada continues to bless and to guide us.[3]

To Act with Economic Fairness

Economics is part of God's concern for his creation. During the rise of the Social Gospel movement in the 1930s and 1940s, some evangelicals argued that the country's economy was outside the scope of biblical concerns.

Old Testament theology disagrees. There was to be an integration of money management with God's redemption. The exodus from Egypt included a plan God had for the people: politically, they were freed from a tyrant; socially, they were lifted from outside interference in family life; spiritually, they were called to leave aside foreign gods and enter into a full covenant with God; economically, they were unchained from forced labour.

In the promised land, there was an equitable distribution of acreages but, given the variability of the terrain, "it did not mean that every family should have the same, but that every family should have enough for economic viability."[4] After receiving land, families varied in how successfully they managed their enterprises. Some became wealthy, while others ended up selling themselves into service in other households just to survive. For those who lost out on economic well-being, there was special concern and protection, along with other groups such as widows, orphans, immigrant aliens, and Levites (Exod. 21:2–6; Deut. 15:12–18).

Overriding it all was a long-term vision and hope that there would be a day when "every man will sit under his own vine and under his own fig tree" (Micah 4:4). Ezekiel holds out the promise that aliens with no land will be given secure tenure and will be able to share in the inheritance given by God.

There are obligations and responsibilities placed on people, but these only support the inclusive nature of economics in the ordering of God's good creation.

THE TASK OF CHRISTIAN CITIZENS

Christians are called to alert government to fulfill its mandate. A secular state, insensitive to God's rule, will miss warnings which a Christian—sensitive to biblical values, it is hoped—sees and understands.

To Remind the Nation It Is Under God

What a challenge in a secular, materialistic world. If Christian faith is relegated to the private enclaves of personal living and church life, how can a Christian remind the nation of where it sits in relationship to God's creation? It can't. That's why Christians are called to live out the life of Christ, reminding the nation that the sovereign Lord is Lord of all. These reminders take place in hospital operating rooms, union halls, day-care centres, courtrooms, cabs of tractor-trailers, fishing trawlers, factories, and election-campaign headquarters—yes, in every part of life. Our lives speak of Christ's lordship wherever we are.

To Remind the Nation That It Is Not Forever

Each country has its own history, which means there is a point in its past when it began. If so, it must be acknowledged that there may be a time in the future when it will change from its present.

Nations have their history. They travel far from their early beginnings. Compared with our early years, today we live in a very different national climate. Amid deep fragmentation and hostilities, various groups have made new political, social, and economic arrangements. Canada, now in closer economic union with the United States, continues to change. What will that do to our future political and social arrangements? We do not know.

We do know that God uses nations as he does people. North America has been a "spiritual breadbasket" for the church worldwide. Its citizens have been characterized by their generosity. Canada's image and presence as a mediator and peacekeeper is one that I wish to maintain. Our effectiveness is appreciated by nations the world over.

Again, this is not categorical evidence of God's will; it is merely what I believe. However, God's will is not detached from what Christians do. We do not live our lives without regard for our feelings and beliefs.

To Remind Our Nation We Are Part of Something Larger

Jonah learned that his nation, Israel, was not all there was to God's world. The real story of Jonah is not the large fish. Jonah refused to go to Nineveh because he did not believe God should have any interest in a nation so evil. To Jonah's chagrin, God not only was interested in Nineveh, but spared it from punishment.

Nationalism has its downside. It can create a preoccupation with one's own nation to the exclusion of others. This leads to wars, disputes, and flagrant disregard for the fact that we are all on this planet together. Canada, as a smaller, less significant nation than its southern neighbour, tends to be more conscious of other nations. Being small by standards of population, and given our history and the development of our national character, in spirit we tend to be more like the Swedes and Swiss: not big enough to seriously offend or hurt others. While we end up with an inferiority complex, it does help us see beyond our own borders.

To Remind Its People that Political Service Is a High Calling

A group that is unfortunately constantly put down and derided is politicians and government staff. Some say politicians bring it on themselves. We hear opposing parties accusing the ruling party of using its power for personal benefit; after the next election, if one of the opposition parties wins, it is accused, in turn, of doing what the former government did. This only feeds our cynicism. It is here that the Christian community can act.

What can be done to restore the high office of political leadership to credibility and effectiveness? First, the church must believe that public leadership is a calling from God and requires the most skilled and prepared people. Cynicism about political leadership (which I hear too often from Christians) will not encourage gifted Christians to offer themselves for political service. It is important that we see the profound need there is for Christians to view such a task as worthy of their lives and commitment.

Once Christians are elected, they don't need rebuke, but encouragement, as they learn what it means to be faithful to the gospel in the cut and thrust of political life. Churches offer training courses, manuals, and refresher courses on missionary service, but where do you ever see courses in preparing leaders to serve in political life? To guide this country, we need to prepare people for public service. We think missionary service is a priority, and I don't know of a more needy "mission field" than our political centres.

I find that people in political life are deeply committed to serve and to be effective and honest in their dealings. Our current parliamentary system makes it difficult for members to hold publicly to their personal views. Party solidarity, enforced by our entrenched party-caucus system, expects its members to abide by party policy, whether or not that policy accords with the personal beliefs of the parliamentarian.

During their political term, our politicians need encouragement. Once elected, most are startled by what happens. One Senator said,

> When I was running for office, people encouraged me, but when I got to Washington, not only did they forget I was here, but they seemed to forget I, too, was human and needed encouragement. They only called me when they were angry or wanted something.

To Remind the Nation that There Are Consequences

We cannot blind ourselves to our national failures and sins. As God has a purpose for a nation, it is not exempt from the law that sin will inevitably be found out.

Massive national debt is a clear and frightening example. Regardless of which government we blame, as citizens we are finally responsible. In democratic societies, we elected governments. And the money was spent on us. From time to time there is an attempt to curtail the spending, but too often those affected by a cutback cry out, "Not in my back yard." That sin we will pay for, either in this generation or in the next.

This prophetic role of examining a society's weaknesses and sins and speaking with power and conviction is important for Christians. Without this insight, a nation can quickly become absorbed in its immediate self-interests, blinded to the consequences of its sins.

IS A CHRISTIAN POLITICAL PARTY NEEDED?

Even after being with Jesus for three years, the disciples quarreled as to who would rule in the future kingdom. After Constantine, the church was enmeshed in the business of running the political order. The reformers—Luther, Calvin, and Menno Simons—worked out their own views of the relationship between church and state. European countries from time to time have had parties called Christian, Christian Democrat or some variation. Today in North America, especially since the rise of the "Religious Right" in the United States, the debate has taken on a North American flavor. A question asked by some is, does a nation need a party designated as Christian?

The concept of such an entity as a "Christian" party is not without difficulties. Who defines what it means to be Christian? Will such a party be Roman Catholic or Protestant, liberal or conservative? Who decides the biblical economic policy? Will it be socialist or free enterprise? Is there even a single biblical view of economics, child care, or the military? Or do Christians hold many views on all of these subjects, each of them claiming to originate in biblical principles?

Another concern is the use of the label "Christian" either to define a party or to name it. In effect, such a label makes an explicit claim on all that such a party does. Inevitably the party—notwithstanding the good intent of its people to be Christian—will do something that dishonors the name of Christ.

There is also a danger that Christians will feel obligated to join that party. Party leaders will experience an involuntary antagonism from Christians who do not share their political vision and views. But the question of whether we need a designated "Christian" political party continues to call for answers.

Does the Bible Call for Such a Party?

The simple answer is no. Nowhere in the teachings of Jesus, the history of the early church, or the texts of any of the New Testament writers is there even an oblique reference to the need or the call for a political party or a ruling government that is Christian.

In the Old Testament, God first established a theocracy from which society was ruled, then a monarchy whereby rule was undertaken by a designated king. Though everything Jesus says is in a sense political, there is no call for the people of God to set up political parties. That is not to say they should not. (Neither did Jesus tell us to build schools or church buildings.) There is no implicit or explicit command or instruction in the New Testament that mandates a "Christian" political party.

Would Having a "Christian" Party Do Any Good?

There are several reasons to justify establishing a Christian party. First, it would bring together Christians from various church denominations, including those who might normally interact only with those of their own Christian group. As well, it would provide a political setting for people gifted and interested in thinking through their independent philosophy.

It is much like the Christian school movement. The goal of alternative Christian schools is to provide an environment in which children can learn about life and develop skills, nurtured by a Christian world view. The assumption is that once trained, graduates will be equipped to move into the marketplace with a solid view of their faith. The same argument could be made for a "Christian" political party. If the intent is to nurture people in the specific field of public leadership and to equip them to serve Christ and the church in the political world, then the forming of such an enterprise may prove to be of value.

A Christian party has another benefit as well: it would alert the political system that there are citizens whose policies rise out of different values and objectives. A political caucus system makes it difficult for elected members to speak publicly on anything but the party line. A separate party would permit the public expression of a point of view that not even Christians in other parties can speak to.

But there is a pragmatic side to this question. People have only so much time and money, and they want to know whether or not such an investment will bear any fruit. In Canada, given our diversity, it would be very difficult for such a party to win an election. Provincially, electoral success would depend on the demography of the population and its inclination to move to non-mainline parties, or the presence of a strong, Christian community who believes that separating from the mainstream parties is a more faithful witness of their faith.

The creation of a Christian political party might have benefits to both the Christian community and the society, but there is no call from the Scriptures for such.

BUILDING A VISION FOR YOUR COUNTRY

How does a Christian, recognizing the varied political, regional, and religious points of view, construct a vision for one's country?

In developing a vision, there are two primary considerations: that God is honoured by the activities of the nation, and that people within the nation are enabled to fulfill their calling. This is not to imply that all will become Christian or that the nation is synonymous with Christ's kingdom. It is to recognize that there is an accrued blessing to a nation whose understanding of creation and life is shaped and guided by a Christian world view. The psalmist said, "Blessed is the nation whose God is the Lord" (Ps. 33:12).

Government, as a creation of God, is the means for a nation to operate. Therefore, those who have the task to govern do so by the authority given by God.

Joseph was given the task of governing Egypt following his spectacular rise to power. Years later, Moses was called to oversee, lead, and govern the Hebrews trapped by slavery in Egypt. Moses, in leading his collection of tribes, appointed

> capable men from all Israel and made them leaders of the people, officials over thousands, hundreds, fifties and tens. They served as judges for the people at all times (Exod. 18:25–26).

As they moved out to Canaan, Moses wrote laws and regulations under which this nation, now wandering but soon to be in residence, would operate.

A brief overview of the history of Israel makes clear the importance of a governmental system. The names of many leaders come to mind: Joshua, who followed Moses and settled the Hebrews into their new land; Gideon, who, although frightened by the enemy, responded to the need for protection of his people, defeated the enemy and went on to give leadership; Deborah, a wise and motivating leader; various kings, the best known being David, under whose rule the country was unified and Jerusalem became the centre in which Jehovah was worshiped. The anointing ceremony under the instituted monarchy was a public statement that God had established the lines of authority to ensure the possibility of harmony.

Paul makes it clear that the role of government is part of God's creation and social order. "The authorities that exist have been established by God...For he is God's servant to do you good" (Rom. 13:1, 4). And "for by him all things were created: ...whether thrones or powers or rulers or authorities; all things were created by him and for him" (Col. 1:16).

THE KINGDOM

The last of the beatitudes is:

Blessed [privileged or happy] are you when men revile you and persecute you and utter all kinds of evil against you falsely on my account. Rejoice and be glad for your reward is great in heaven, for so men persecuted the prophets who were before you.

In the first eight beatitudes, Jesus creates an understanding of what his kingdom is by showing us its construct: the poor receive the kingdom; mourners are comforted; the meek inherit the earth; those who hunger for righteousness will be filled; the merciful are shown mercy; the pure in heart see God; the peacemakers are called the sons of God; and the persecuted inherit the kingdom.

In this final one, Christ shifts by calling us to be part of the agony of the kingdom in this world. First, Jesus told us what the kingdom is. Now he tells us how we are expected to behave by staying in the world and not escaping from it. This is radical. Jesus calls the church to think and behave in ways that are out of sync with the prevailing culture.

Observe the interests that essentially preoccupy Christians. Then set them alongside Christ's kingdom and ask what they have in common. Do our personal and public attitudes toward leadership and people in need match the guidelines given by Jesus?

This kingdom of heaven is not that which will come only in the future. Christ has already come. The coming of the King at the end of the age does not imply that the kingdom is not alive and active today. Robert Bellah, known for his critique of society in *Habits of the Heart,* said,

> If we do not recover the language and practice of Christianity, if we do not discover that the Kingdom of heaven is our only true home, the place that defines our most essential identity, then not only can we not contribute to a genuine pluralism, but we will be lost in the wilderness of decayed traditions and vulnerable to the combination of modernity's suicidal infatuation with power, the exact opposite of the Gospel message.[5]

At the heart of the matter is a need for Christians to be radical in their understanding and in the outworking of the gospel of Jesus. We do not need Christians spouting more political theories. Our citizens need to hear the language of the gospel. The gospel offers a radical presence that is not merely words on paper but the way of life of Jesus of Nazareth and his prescription for our minds, hearts and behaviour.

Fear or anger at a society adrift from biblical truth will do little to renew it, and for certain will not bring a witness of Christ's creative and restorative power. Instead, I suggest that we must seek a new understanding and strategy of engagement.

ASSUMPTIONS OF ENGAGEMENT

As we seek to be change agents in this pluralistic world, there are assumptions we bring to the task: spiritual weapons; being a neighbour; a sacrificial spirit; learning from the Spirit of Truth; seeing widely and with a courageous spirit. The apostle Paul sets the context of our witness by reminding us we are temples of God (1 Cor. 6:19). We do not engage our culture equipped only with our talents, education, personality and personal goals. We are not to live as if we are accountable only to ourselves. We are Christ's by the offering of salvation, and we live in a community that calls on us to be accountable to other Christians. We are united with Christ in our witness. As we begin the witness, we are anointed with the Spirit.

Consider these fruits of his Spirit: love, joy, peace, patience, kindness, goodness, faithfulness, gentleness, and self-control (Gal. 5:22, 23). They are like a mantle. They speak to how we are to conduct ourselves, how our attitudes are to rule us, and how they might modify our style as we give witness of Christ.

As we engage our world, we are to be ruled by Christ's loving Spirit. Jesus traveled through the community, preaching the good news with mercy: "When he saw the crowds, he had compassion on them, because they were harassed and helpless, like sheep without a shepherd" (Matt. 9:39). It is too easy to be caught in anger against those who are destructive and confrontational. I understand that only too well. But an instinctive reaction of anger is not right, as the next story reminds us.

I was part of a small group asked to appear before a committee on abortion. I knew our views would antagonize some. As we prayed before the meeting, one of our members asked the Lord to give us the spirit of gentleness and humility. As the meeting progressed, tough questions were asked. I could feel the heat rise. But in the answer we gave, I sensed a gentle spirit. At the close, a Member of Parliament opposed to our views said, "I never knew evangelicals cared so much about the well-being of both women and the unborn." I suppose she had heard only our strident expression of concern about the lives of the unborn, and not that of our deep love and concern for mothers as well. Paul wrote, "By the meekness and gentleness of Christ, I appeal to you..." (2 Cor. 10:1).

At the same time, being fair, just and compassionate does not imply simply accepting other views without examination. Social commentator Don Posterski puts it well: "Pluralism without discernment can lead to a convictionless culture."[6] Determining to find a way to live peaceably should lead to a tough critique of the public positions put forward by others. For example, homosexual groups lobbying for what they regard as their rights require from Christians more than

either an outright rejection in the name of truth or a wholesale acceptance in the name of compassion. The call for "fairness" from an opposing position in any argument does not mean that the logic of that position is unassailable. What is required is to discern the difference
between treating homosexuals fairly and opening the door to a profoundly unbiblical view of sexuality, resulting in the breaking down of
our understanding of marriage and family. Discerning the difference is
essential to being both fair and helpful in developing public policy.

To the public arena we bring weapons, but weapons not common
to the world. "For though we live in the world, we do not wage war as
the world does. The weapons we fight with are not the weapons of the
world" (2 Cor. 10:3, 4). The Spirit places into our hands God's weapons.
How quick we are to fight words with words or political power with
political power. Those who led the Social Gospel Movement of the early
twentieth century, while concerned about bringing in the kingdom,
resorted to the same implements of political warfare used by those they
opposed. Public protest and strikes, electing politicians, and eventually
starting their own party were the only means they saw of instituting
kingdom principles. Although some of them surely did, little does one
read of them praying and seeking God's will. In the end, we are called to
acknowledge that our ways are not God's ways.

We also live in the Spirit by being a neighbour. When I come in
contact with a neighbour (the story of the Good Samaritan reminds
us that a neighbour is anyone we meet), I am compelled by the great
commandment to love my neighbour as myself (Luke 10:27).

Central to Christ is the sacrificial spirit. Discomfort and incon-
venience are not to be seen as evidence that we are out of sync with
the Spirit. Indeed, the opposite may be true. The apostle Peter put it
this way:

> Dear friends, do not be surprised at the painful trial you are
> suffering, as though something strange were happening to
> you. But rejoice that you participate in the sufferings of
> Christ... (1 Peter 4:12-13).

Our society is so antiseptic in its ways that suffering is seen as
something to be avoided. Too easily we connect our society's fear of

suffering to personal living, and so construe our experiences so that discomfort or pain in our Christian lives is to be avoided.

We are linked to the church. As members of the household of faith, we do not live to ourselves. Luke notes Peter's first defense on the day of Pentecost: "Then Peter stood up with the eleven..." (Acts 2:14). An individualistic spirit does not fit. We are in community, accountable to each other. Not only does that give us encouragement, but it refines our words and actions. None of us is a John Wayne, striding off across the prairies, gun in hand, epitomizing the ideal of individualism. We do not live in isolation. What we do or say affects the rest of the church. And because it does, we are accountable.

The Spirit of Truth is one name for the Holy Spirit (John 14:17). Learning the facts and truth is indispensable. Misinformation is unacceptable. Our arguments, our Christian community and the One we serve are discredited by untruth.

Germans have a wonderfully descriptive word, *Weltanschauung*, meaning "comprehensive philosophy of life." It reminds me of Jesus, who noted that his disciples were caught up in their own narrow and self-serving issues. "Open your eyes and look at the fields! They are ripe for harvest" (John 4:35). In other words, don't be caught up in just looking at the field around you. Take a look beyond your fences! An issue is not isolated. It is part of a larger reality. For example, Francis Schaeffer, along with then surgeon general of the United States, Dr. Everett Koop, warned that abortion was just the beginning of the life issue. Soon would come euthanasia and "mercy killing," he warned. This is a world-seeing Spirit in which we perceive how life is interconnected. They noted that once you start on the slippery slope of caring more for the mother than for the unborn, it's not far to the assumption that the elderly or severely handicapped also have little in life, and so why not end their lives, too?

The Holy Spirit is world-seeing and end-seeing. Writer Stephen R. Covey suggests that, in analyzing the importance of today's work, you should visualize standing at your own funeral, hearing your own eulogy. What would I want to be said at that time? This helps me more carefully decide what I do today as I live today with the end in view. For a Christian, the end is a certain and joyous reality. This can keep us from being caught up in or consumed by a single issue, without regard for how it might play out in the future.

A key assumption of our approach is humility. But our driving concern for self neutralizes our efforts. Pride, more quickly than almost any other contrary spirit, will destroy effective kingdom work. I learned that even when I believed my views were consistent with the Scriptures, my attitude was wrong, keeping me from doing good.

One day I was invited by the late Barbara Frum, then host of CBC's television program, *The Journal,* to participate in a public debate on AIDS. Around the table were a number of medical and social-welfare professionals. My role was to ask the religious questions. Across the table was Al, a schoolteacher dying from AIDS. I knew my calling was to speak truth into this debate. But I was not ready for what occurred.

During the early part of the roundtable discussion, I looked at Al. Instead of seeing his failings, it was as if the Spirit used his eyes as a mirror and I saw myself. What I saw was not attractive: pride, hatred, revulsion, self-righteousness. I struggled through the taping. I knew I had been found out. I had brought no humility to the discussion. Spiritual pride ruled. After the taping, I walked around the table, put my arms around Al, and told him I loved him. It was my way of confessing my sin of pride and restoring a spirit of humility. Without that spirit, our works and words become clashing cymbals. I continue to affirm a biblical view of sexuality, because it is best for our country and because I believe such an understanding is true. But my heart has been changed.

The spirit of fear and the desire to dominate will also destroy effective kingdom work. Henri Nouwen has good things to say about this in *The Way of the Heart.*[7] We "become conspirators with the darkness" when we give in to our dependence on the "responses of our social milieu." Having the comfort of knowing we fit in and are approved of by the majority can become a "compulsion." When we think that we no longer fit in, when we no longer have society's approval, we become angry and afraid because we are being deprived of that which we have become dependent on.

The Spirit of Christ is also a courageous spirit. In resisting the status quo, we refuse to be intimidated by opposing forces.

For God did not give us a spirit of timidity, but a spirit of power, love and of self-discipline. So do not be ashamed to testify about our Lord or ashamed of me his prisoner (2 Tim. 1:7, 8).

The very act of courage will bring others out of hiding. It will model to Christians how to give a public witness.

HOW TO WORK

Mindful that we are surrounded by the Spirit and his truth, we don't need to back away from engaging our culture. But in order to so engage, there are some principles to help us on the way. Some of those principles I first learned through open-line radio and television shows. One early program featured a doctor who had become famous for promoting abortion on demand. I happened to be in a distant city from where the program originated and the studio where the doctor sat.

As I waited for the phone link-up, I silently asked for wisdom. I was impressed with three ideas: (1) Be kind. Railing against him discredits the One we serve and ends up making my counterpart into a hero. (2) Do not try to win the entire argument today. Critique the foundational arguments and show their inconsistencies. (3) Do not use Bible verses in this public forum. Yes, I believe in the Bible, but to use it with those who do not believe is to invite their scorn and repudiation of the Bible. Instead, use biblical ideas expressed in nonbiblical language.

As I take calls on radio or television, I visualize being at a round-table with people from various faiths and insights: some hostile to Christian faith, some ignorant, most uninterested, and a few open to ideas. My task is to engage them in a thoughtful, interesting, and challenging debate on the meaning of Christian faith. It is a round-table expression of public opinion. My call is to present ideas in such a way as to alert people to Christ, to challenge their false assumptions and remind them of the cultural gods they serve. There are many tables around which our culture sits: education, economic, medical and legal, to name just a few. With the image of the table in mind, there are basic steps in making a public witness.

STEPS TO SITTING AT THE TABLE

1. Get your facts straight

For a number of years, gullible Christians in North America were hoodwinked into writing to the U.S. Federal Commission on Communication, calling on the government to reject Madalyn O'Hair's alleged attempt to push Christian radio off the air. First, she has never worked to do this. Though it sounds like something she might have done, akin to her objection to the Lord's Prayer in public schools, she has not. Well-meaning people copy petitions in the effort to do something good, often all to waste, for one reason: they have not checked out the facts. This was an enormous waste of time and energy. The gospel is discredited when, in arguing for even a good idea, one works with the wrong set of facts.

2. Decide what the real issue is

If you are asking for parental involvement in the education of your child, do not allow yourself to get caught up in an argument over something like sex education. If the issue is to permit parents to have a voice in what is done in the classroom, stick with that issue. Raising other issues distracts and raises the wall of resistance. Deal with other issues at another time.

3. Digest other arguments and views

Take time to know and understand the other points of view. It will surprise opponents to know that you have taken time to understand their concerns. Knowing the essence of their view not only forces you to come to grips with what they believe, but provides you with a basis for response.

4. Test your approach with others

It is easy to assume that you know the arguments and have captured the essence of the debate; then, in the actual encounter, the arguments seem weak. What has gone wrong? You have not sufficiently refined your arguments in advance to test your rationale and logic in public.

5. Meet the major players

If your presentation is before the city council, meet the councilors earlier. If the issue is with a teacher, find out who that teacher is as a person.

6. Learn how the system works

Each community, governmental or political entity has its own way of functioning. Get to know how the municipal, provincial or national system operates.

7. Be at the table

Decisions are made at places and meetings. If there is occasion for input, or if there is opportunity for membership or participation, you must find the time and place and get permission to attend. Often a Christian voice is lost because the logistics have been neglected.

8. Build coalitions

Policy-makers make decisions within certain deadlines. The variety of interests, views, and opinions must be analyzed and a decision made. From the varied positions, a final position will be hammered out. The issue may not be as much one of truth as of process. There will be pressures on the decision-makers to come up with answers and solutions that best fit the majority of views. In expressing your views, seek ways of developing liaisons with others. Don't compromise on the fundamental issues, but combine strengths in order to influence the decision in the right direction.

9. Learn the appropriate role of compromise

We have scrambled from interacting with those of opposing views because of the fear of compromise. But all of us, be it in our marriages or in personal relationships must be willing to reduce our demands or expectations. Likewise, in public life one must modify expectations and demands in dealing in public matters. The line to draw is not whether or not to compromise, but on what grounds.

The most tragic moment in my experience in working on public policy was during the federal debate on abortion in the early 1990s. The proposed abortion bill was being opposed by most pro-life organizations because in their view it did not go far enough in protecting the unborn. I saw it another way. There were essentially three approaches the government could take on abortion legislation. The first was based on gestation: that is, abortion could be allowed up to a certain number of weeks. This was a mechanical view of life. And how would the law decide at what week to disallow abortions? The second approach was to permit no abortions, which was unacceptable to the majority of Canadians and stood no chance of being approved. The third approach, which was adopted in this bill, affirmed life as existing from the point of conception, but it did allow abortion in a number of exceptional circumstances.

Although the bill allowed too many exceptions, I supported it on the basis that it was public policy pointed in the right direction and, over time, the number of exceptions could be reduced. The right principle was in place, even if some of the specifics were flawed.

Here the principle of the right of the unborn was affirmed. There was no compromise of principles. The conviction was retained. In the end, the bill was defeated in the Senate by one vote. And so, today, we are the only country in the Western world that has no legal restrictions on abortion—at least in part because those who wanted to do right failed to understand the legitimate place of compromise in the writing of public policy.

10. Finally, do not be weary in well-doing

The shaping of an idea and then the moving of it into the laws and policies of our society does not happen overnight. Remember that the takeover by ruling ideologies occurred over many years. If your concern is worth the effort, then use the opportunity and structure to pursue your agenda and goal.

WHAT WILL NOT WORK

I am called to follow Christ in all of life. This I bring to any discussion. Sitting around the table of pluralism, I am challenged to remain faithful to the gospel and yet work in a cordial manner. Given that a dominant Christian presence is gone, we are called, regardless of the setting, to be faithful. So in this new setting, what will not work to advance a biblical vision? I suggest there are three positions that will not work.

1. Imposing

The first is to try to impose the values of Christian faith on an uninterested, hostile or nonbelieving public. Christians often ask, "Why must we always give in to others when our country was founded on Christian principles? Do we not have the right to insist that these be retained?"

There is one major response. "What would Jesus do? Is that the way of Christ?" For example, even though we have experienced centuries of the dominance of Christendom in the Western and European communities, does that give us the right to insist that people live the way we have known? I hardly think that conforms to either the Spirit or the ways of Christ.

2. Doing nothing

It is difficult to engage with those who are indifferent or hostile to our views or concerns. How easy it is to back away and live my spiritual life within the confines and protection of those who believe as I do. This carries with it a hazard: it allows those forces that have already displaced Christian faith to continue without resistance. If the reshaping of our society holds any interest—even within the belief that the return of Christ is near—then the cost of influencing the direction of our society is high. Quite simply, if our will is silent, the will of others prevails. However, beyond the issue of cause/effect there is a matter of obedience: Christ calls us to be "in the world," even though we are not to be "of the world."

3. Building barriers

Another response is to build barriers against those whom you oppose. This does create a certain comfort by excluding opposing views from your domain, but it accomplishes nothing. Public policies are written and implemented by people within an environment of secularism. This we must not forget. To access that decision-making process and to achieve public policies that reflect a biblical vision for life requires not the building of barriers, but the tearing down of walls.

THE UNITY OF MANY TONGUES

On the day of Pentecost, the gospel was preached in the many tongues of those who had gathered in Jerusalem for the Hebrew celebration. The message of Christ was not tied to the immediate culture, nor was it heard only in the Greek language. It was for all people, within the sphere of their own languages. What a spectacular display of God's will that his message was heard in every culture. God is not against culture; it serves as a vehicle of life. The dividing line we too often cross over is making culture the final word on truth. All cultures are circumscribed by both space and time. Each country has many ideas and views to offer the world. Could it be that we become so shaped by the difficulties of our land that our thinking is stunted and our language curtailed?

By way of my role of leadership among evangelicals, I had the opportunity of meeting with senior political leaders. It was one of those days when I was scheduled to meet with the prime minister. When one has forty minutes with the prime minister, you are careful to work out the agenda.

This I had done with our committee on national affairs. We had gone over what questions I would ask, what I would propose and those issues for which we would ask for his support.

I was early for the meeting, so the staff invited me to wait in a side room. With a few minutes before the meeting, I took out the Scriptures. Given that I was doing a study of Daniel, I absent-mindedly opened to Daniel and began to flip through the pages. There was nothing in particular I was looking for, but my eyes fell to Daniel 11:1(NASB): "In the first year of Darius the Mede, I rose to be an encouragement and protection for him."

I sensed the Spirit saying, drop your agenda and bless the king.

My first thought was, if I do, what will the committee on national affairs say?

A few minutes later I was called in. I sat with the prime minister for some time, chatting about life, going over some of his concerns and reflecting on the needs and mood of the country.

Then he asked, "Brian, what's your agenda?"

I gulped and then said, "Mr. Prime Minister, I don't have an agenda." He looked surprised. Most of his appointments are about groups asking the government for something.

"No," I said. "Rather I'm here to be an encouragement to you. I'd like to take a moment and reflect on the call the Scriptures make to leadership."

I took out my Bible and opened it to Romans 13, and noted what Paul said the government was to do. I referred to Colossians 1:16 in which all things, including thrones, powers, rulers, and authorities are Christ's creation.

After talking for some time on these texts and what they might mean, at the end of my forty minutes I had prayer and then left. But I left with no assurance that what I had done was the right thing to do.

Of course the committee on national affairs wanted to know the prime minister's response to our agenda. They were not pleased with my response.

The following week as I boarded an airplane, and was looking for my assigned seat, I heard my name. Turning, I saw it was the minister of justice. We had a few minutes before the flight would leave, so I stopped for a moment to chat.

Then he surprised me. "Brian, what in the world happened with you and the prime minister last week?"

"How did you know?" I asked. I was startled by the question. First I thought the meeting was private and then I was afraid that what I had said had offended the prime minister.

"Oh, he told us in the party meeting this morning about your visit."

"Was there anything wrong?" I asked.

"Not at all," the minister responded. "He told us about your Bible study and prayer and said it was one of the most encouraging meetings he has had in a long time. He ended up by saying, if we ignore the evangelical Christian community then our country is the loser."

What a lesson to be learned about the ways God enters into human life and government. That one meeting opened more doors for conversation than all the petitions or briefs we could have written.

Over all that I love and appreciate about being a citizen of my country, I know that Christ calls me to understand the language of God's Word. That language calls me to rise above the spirit of the age and be guided by the Spirit of the Ages.

CALLED TO SPEAK GOD'S LANGUAGE

Language is the essential means whereby beliefs and feelings are expressed. In the Christian tradition, words are of great importance. God spoke and Creation became a reality. God spoke to Moses and gave the Ten Commandments. The prophets spoke God's word and people were expected to understand and obey. Jesus Christ is called "the Word." The Bible is a written document that conveys truth. For Christians, the notion of words as the conveyors of truth is critical.

An important question is, does Christ make any difference in the way I view my nation? Are my self-interests so overriding as to exclude the fundamental question of what Christ expects of us? Have the resentments gone so deep in our lives as to cut us off from any ability to think and ask the biblical questions?

We must ask, what is there about the life of the church that would attract our society to ask it for guidance? Does the church have something of substance to say to the larger culture, or has it become just another noisy group within a society that wants more and more?

Responding to the questions of our culture requires a new orientation. Now that the overriding assumptions and evident Christian influences within my nation are a thing of the past, at times I feel like a foreigner. We become like the exiled Hebrews trying to sing in Babylon. In exile they were asked to sing the songs of Zion—that is, Jerusalem. The psalmist wrote: "By the rivers of Babylon we sat and wept, when we remembered Zion. There on the poplars we hung our harps, for there our captors asked us for songs, our tormentors demanded songs of joy; they said, 'Sing us one of the songs of Zion!'" The singer asked, "How can we sing the songs of the LORD while in a foreign land?" (Ps. 137:1–4).

The answer? You can't.

Exiled from Israel, missing the familiar sounds of the homeland and the great celebrations and feasts of the Jewish calendar, the psalmist found it impossible to sing the songs of Zion in Babylon. To sing the songs of the past in a society paganized by its rejection of the transcendent and secularized by its laws and policies is impossible.

The poet could not sing the songs of his past culture, that is, Zion or Jerusalem. But he could have sung the songs of the King. You can sing the songs of faith anywhere. Could it be that in our longing for the seemingly pleasant days of the past, in which the common song of faith could be sung in the public square, we are trying to sing the cultural songs of Zion instead of the liberating songs of the King?

We can rail against the incompetence of leaders in all spheres of public life; we can decry the moral bankruptcy of their policies and plans; we can go so far as to call for their downfall. But is that song any different from what we hear on our roads and in our squares? The songs of the cultural past, as nice as they seem in memory, will not be listened to today. Does that mean that the message of God is irrelevant today? No. But the song must be that of faith and truth. It must come from the heart of the King, and not from culture. The culture of the church is often irrelevant to the message of the kingdom of Christ and becomes a barrier, preventing people from understanding and entering the kingdom.

And who will sing the songs of the King? Will they be heard in the arena of political sniping? Will the melody line be heard in the harsh sounds of anti-this and anti-that? If people who claim to be of the King do not sing the King's songs, then who will?

The tragedy in many countries is not primarily political fragmentation or disagreements over native land claims, forms of taxation, or even public leadership. It is that the church has stopped singing the song of biblical faith and life in the public square. Or do we sing off key? By not saying that only the truth will set you free, we have a society that hopes life will get better. We have layered our message with so much of the world that our tune is neither distinctive nor even noticed.

We know that Christian faith has profoundly shaped our language, vision, institutions, and policies. But with the radical shift in cultural assumptions, many Christians wonder if there is any value in expending effort in attempting to reinstate Christian norms. Some will ask, "Is it possible?" Others, "Is it worthwhile?" And still others, "Does Christ even call for it?"

A rabbi in Britain supported Christianity as the predominant religion in the public schools in England. It was his conviction that it would be better to be a Jew in a Christian country than to be a Jew in a secular country. Then he added a proviso, "provided it is a Christian country."

He went on to tell the story of a rabbi who gained an audience with the czar and the czarina to ask their assistance about the problem of anti-Semitism in nineteenth-century Russia. The czarina rudely commented, "If they want peace, then let the Jews become Christians."

The rabbi thought for a moment and replied, "No, let the Christians become Christians, then we shall all have peace."

What we have to offer is Jesus Christ, not a mimicry of the surrounding culture. He calls us to see life through the lens of eternity and not the demands of time. We must hear and learn to speak the language of his creation and his redeeming call.

Notes

Chapter 1: Why Twentieth-Century Christians Withdrew from Political Life

1. Os Guinness, *The Dust of Death* (Downers Grove, IL: InterVarsity, 1973), p. 8.
2. Grant, *The Church in the Canadian Era* (Burlington, Ontario: Welch Publishing Company Inc., 1988) pp. 102–103.
3. George Grant, *Technology and Empire* (Toronto: Anansi, 1969), p. 114.
4. Mark Noll, Nathan Hatch, and George Marsden, *The Search for Christian America* (Colorado Springs: Helmers & Howard, 1989), p. 31.

Chapter 2: What the Old Testament Says about Nation Building

1. These three windows or hermeneutical methods through which the Old Testament can be interpreted come from the writings of Christopher J.W. Wright, *An Eye for an Eye* (Downers Grove, IL: InterVarsity, 1983). Note Chapter 4, "Economics and the Land," especially pp. 88–102.
2. See Revelation 12:7 and Ezekiel 28. "Lucifer" is a Latin word referring to the Hebrew word for "morning star," used by Isaiah: "How you have fallen from heaven, O morning star, son of the dawn! You have been cast down to the earth, you who once laid low the nations" (Isa. 14:12).
3. Wright, *An Eye for an Eye*, p. 72.
4. *Baker Encyclopedia of the Bible*, ed. Walter A. Elwell (Grand Rapids,

MI: Baker Book House, 1988), vol. 1, p. 243.

    5. Wright, *An Eye for an Eye*, p. 106.

    6. Genesis 25:12–18 lists Ishmael's descendants. "North Arab genealogists trace their ancestry back to Ishmael," *Baker Encyclopedia of the Bible*, vol. 1, p. 145.

Chapter 3: Jesus and Politics

    1. John Stott, *Decisive Issues Facing Christians Today* (Old Tappan, NJ: Fleming H. Revell, 1990), p. 11.

    2. John Bright, *The Kingdom of God* (Nashville: Abingdon, 1953), p. 18.

    3. Ibid., p. 217.

Chapter 4: Thinking with a Christian World View

    1. Harry Blamires, *The Christian Mind* (Ann Arbor: Servant Books, 1963), p. 4.

    2. Richard J. Mouw, *Politics and the Biblical Drama* (Grand Rapids, MI: Eerdmans, 1976), p. 10.

    3. For help on this question of the use of Israel as metaphor for nationhood, be advised of the cautions expressed in Mark Noll, Nathan Hatch, and George Marsden, *The Search for Christian America* (Colorado Springs: Helmers & Howard, 1989).

    4. Seymour Lipset, *Continental Divide* (New York: Routledge, 1990), p. 77.

    5. Michael Cassidy, *The Passing Summer* (London: Hodder & Stoughton, 1989), p. 101.

Chapter 5: Lessons from the Past: Christians and Rome

    1. Glenn Tinder, *The Political Meaning of Christianity* (New York: HarperCollins, 1991). Note the prologue on the prophetic role of the church.

    2. Richard A. Todd, *God and Caesar*, ed. R.A. Linder, Proceedings of the Conference on Faith and History (Longview, TX, 1971), p. 18.

    3. Os Guinness, *The Dust of Death* (Downers Grove, IL: InterVarsity, 1973), p. 364.

    4. T.M. Parker, *Christianity and the State in the Light of History* (London: A. & C. Black, 1955). p. 28.

    5. Ibid.

6. Ibid., p. 36.
7. Ibid., p. 37.
8. Ibid., p. 39.
9. Ibid., pp. 38-39.
10. Ibid., p. 40.
11. Ibid., p. 59.
12. Robert G. Clouse, Richard V. Pierard, and Edwin M. Yamauchi, *Two Kingdoms: The Church and Culture through the Ages* (Chicago: Moody, 1993), p. 223.
13. Parker, *Christianity and the State in the Light of History*, p. 149.
14. *Luther's Works*, vol. 45 (Philadelphia: Fortress, 1962), pp. 88–92.
15. John Tonkin, *The Church and the Secular Order in Reformation Thought* (New York: Columbia University Press, 1971), p. 145.

Chapter 6: Is Pluralism Just a Modern Babel?

1. Paul Marshall, Secularity and Pluralism Conference, Camp Couchiching, Ontario, 1991.
2. Lesslie Newbigin, *The Gospel in a Pluralist Society* (Grand Rapids, MI: Eerdmans, 1989). The distinction between religious and cultural pluralism comes from this book.
3. Ibid., p. 14.
4. Max L. Stackhouse, *Public Theology and Political Economy: Christian Stewardship in Modern Society* (Grand Rapids, MI: Eerdmans, 1987), p. 159.
5. See Carl F.H. Henry, *Revelation and Authority*, vol. 1 (Waco, TX: Word, 1976), pp. 216ff.
6. Allan Bloom, *The Closing of the American Mind* (New York: Simon & Schuster, 1987), p. 26.
7. Peter Berger, *The Heretical Imperative* (New York: Anchor/Doubleday, 1979), p. 25.
8. Allen C. Guelzo, "Intellectual Sources of Pluralism," in *The Challenge of Religious Pluralism: An Evangelical Analysis and Response*, Proceedings of the Wheaton Theology Conference (Wheaton: Wheaton Graduate School, 1992), p. 89.
9. Ibid., p. 93.
10. Lesslie Newbigin, *Foolishness to the Greeks* (Grand Rapids, MI: Eerdmans, 1986), p. 3.
11. Ibid., p. 7.
12. Donald C. Posterski, *True to You* (Winfield, BC: Wood Lake, 1995), p.161.

13. Newbigin, *Foolishness to the Greeks*, p. 14.

14. John Stott, *Involvement* (Old Tappan, NJ: Fleming H. Revell, 1984), p. 82.

15. Newbigin, *Foolishness to the Greeks*, p. 18.

16. Newbigin, *The Gospel in a Pluralist Society*, p. 17.

17. Corrie Ten Boom, with John and Elizabeth Sherrill, *The Hiding Place* (New York: Chosen, 1971), p. 94.

18. Newbigin, *The Gospel in a Pluralist Society*, p. 159.

Chapter 7: Speaking a New Language

1. H. Richard Niebuhr, *Christ and Culture* (New York: Harper & Row, 1951).

2. John Howard Yoder, *The Politics of Jesus* (Grand Rapids, MI: Eerdmans, 1972), p. 245.

3. 100 Huntley Street broadcast, host, David Mainse, "Salute to Canada," June 20, 1981.

4. Christopher J.H. Wright, *An Eye for an Eye* (Downers Grove, IL: InterVarsity, 1983), p. 77.

5. Robert Bellah, "Christian Faithfulness in a Pluralist World," in *Postmodern Theology*, ed. Frederic B. Burnham (San Francisco: Harper & Row, 1989), p. 91.

6. Don Posterski, *True to You* (Winfield, BC: Wood Lake, 1995), p. 168.

7. Henri Nouwen, *The Way of the Heart* (New York: Ballantine, 1981), pp. 10–12.

Bibliographic Notes

Like most writers, my ideas are either reworkings (conscious or unconscious) of thoughts and ideas of others or a synthesis arrived at by a point of view out of the past bombarded by a new one. To cite a source for each idea here would have cluttered up the page. In cases of direct quotation, I've tried to show the source. However, I want to acknowledge that while the idea of examining what it means to be a Christian within a social/political context derives from my own interest in the subject, I am indebted to many writers for their enormous help.

Chapter 1: Why Twentieth-Century Christians Withdrew from Political Life

There has been little research in this area. My interest began while doing graduate studies at the University of Toronto. My thesis, *The Emergence of Pentecostalism from Sectarianism to Denominationalism* pushed me to think more about my own church experience and why we are so prone to denounce political engagement as being "worldly." However, the question surfaced in ever demanding ways when as president of the Evangelical Fellowship of Canada, I was called on to articulate an evangelical view on a wide-ranging number of subjects. What really pushed me to the wall was when our own community asked me why so few evangelicals were engaged in public and political leadership. I didn't know. So I set about finding the answer. My attempts to make sense of the question resulted in a series of seminars I conducted across Canada, titled *Understanding Our Times*, taken from I

Chronicles 12:32, which describes King David's recruitment of the sons of Issachar, whom the historian describes as having an understanding of the times and knowing what Israel should do. There is a strong correlation to the same development in the United States.

Chapter 2: What the Old Testament Says about Nation Building

Important texts for the Old Testament studies, in searching for roots of New Testament kingdom material, came from Christopher J.W. Wright, *An Eye for an Eye* (Downers Grove, IL: InterVarsity, 1983). I especially found Chapter 4, "Economics and the Land," to be helpful. Note also John Bright, *The Kingdom of God* (Nashville: Abingdon, 1953), and Herman Ridderbos, *The Coming of the Kingdom* (Philadelphia: The Presbyterian and Reformed Publishing Company, 1962).

Chapter 3: Jesus and Politics

Some books to assist in study include John Stott, *Decisive Issues Facing Christians Today* (Old Tappan, NJ: Fleming H. Revell, 1990); John Bright, *The Kingdom of God* (Nashville: Abingdon, 1953); Herman Ridderbos, *The Coming of the Kingdom* (Philadelphia: The Presbyterian and Reformed Publishing Company, 1962); Glenn Tinder, *The Political Meaning of Christianity* (New York: HarperCollins, 1991).

Chapter 4: Thinking with a Christian World View

We are assisted in thinking Christianly by the following: Harry Blamires, *The Christian Mind* (Ann Arbor: Servant, 1963); Vinay K. Samuel, "A Christian Attitude to the State—An Indian Perspective," *Transformation* April/June, 1991; Richard J. Mouw, *Politics and the Biblical Drama* (Grand Rapids, MI: Eerdmans, 1976).

The use of Israel as a metaphor for nationhood is loaded with danger. Mark Noll, Nathan Hatch, and George Marsden, *The Search for Christian America* (Colorado Springs: Helmers & Howard, 1989), and Seymour Lipset, *Continental Divide* (New York: Routledge, 1990), deal with America, while Michael Cassidy, *The Passing Summer* (London: Hodder & Stoughton, 1989), speaks of South Africa.

Chapter 5: Lessons from the Past: Christians and Rome

The relationship of the church and state over the centuries is fascinating and instructive. Of the countless numbers of reference and history books, I found these to be helpful: Glenn Tinder, *The Political Meaning of Christianity* (New York: HarperCollins, 1991); Richard A. Todd, *God and Caesar*, ed. R.A. Linder, Proceedings of the Conference on Faith and History (Longview, TX, 1971); T.M. Parker, *Christianity and the State in the Light of History* (London: A. & C. Black, 1955); Carroll V. Newsom, *The Roots of Christianity* (Englewood Cliffs, NJ: Prentice-Hall, 1979); Robert G. Clouse, Richard V. Pierard, and Edwin M. Yamauchi, *Two Kingdoms: The Church and Culture through the Ages* (Chicago: Moody, 1993); John Tonkin, *The Church and the Secular Order in Reformation Thought* (New York: Columbia University Press, 1971); Jon Butler, *Awash in a Sea of Faith* (Cambridge, MA: Harvard University Press, 1990).

Chapter 6: Is Pluralism Just a Modern Babel?

The distinction between religious pluralism and cultural pluralism comes from Lesslie Newbigin, *The Gospel in a Pluralist Society* (Grand Rapids, MI: Eerdmans, 1989). Other books on pluralism include Richard Mouw and Sander Griffioen, *Pluralism and Horizons* (Grand Rapids, MI: Eerdmans, 1993), a more theoretical treatment that supplies a background to contemporary pluralism is *The Challenge of Religious Pluralism: An Evangelical Analysis and Response*, ed. Allen C. Guelzo, Proceedings of the Wheaton Theology Conference (Wheaton: Wheaton Graduate School, 1992). The lectures begin with a discussion of Ernst Troeltsch, then analyze John Hick's approach and offer suggestions to the church on how it might respond. Also Max L. Stackhouse, *Public Theology and Political Economy: Christian Stewardship in Modern Society* (Grand Rapids, MI: Eerdmans, 1987): Allen C. Guelzo, "Intellectual Sources of Pluralism," *The Challenge of Religious Pluralism: An Evangelical Analysis and Response*, Proceedings of the Wheaton Theology Conference (Wheaton: Wheaton Graduate School, 1992): Allan Bloom, *The Closing of the American Mind* (New York: Simon & Schuster, 1987); Peter Berger, *The Heretical Imperative* (New York: Anchor/Doubleday, 1979): Lesslie Newbigin, *Foolishness to the Greeks* (Grand Rapids, MI: Eerdmans, 1986).

Chapter 7: Speaking a New Language

No study of the church and culture is complete without a look at the classic work, H. Richard Niebuhr, *Christ and Culture* (New York: Harper & Row, 1951). For the Anabaptist view, see John Howard Yoder, *The Politics of Jesus* (Grand Rapids, MI: Eerdmans, 1972). Christopher J.W. Wright, *An Eye for an Eye* (Downers Grove, IL: InterVarsity, 1983), brings together the Old and New of the Scriptures and points the way to a better way of serving out Christ's kingdom. I've been especially encouraged by Richard Mouw's book, *Uncommon Decency* (Downers Grove, IL: InterVarsity, 1991). See especially chapter 3, "Defending Christian Civility." Don Posterski's *True to You* (Winfield, BC: Wood Lake, 1995), is a call to careful and thoughtful Christian attitude and living. And in the end, it is Christians like Henri Nouwen, author of *The Way of the Heart* (New York: Ballantine, 1981), who call us to first love God and then, out of that, love our neighbour.

Index

C

Calvin, John, 33, 113, 152

Cassidy, Michael, 139

Catholic Church see Roman Catholic Church

Charlemagne, 111

Christendom model, 32-34, 107-09, 110,

Christianity

    Contemporary, 16

    culture, 30

    early Church, 102-10, 117, 119

    effective participation in today's world, 30

    Jewish heritage, 38-40, 67-68,

    official religion under Constantine, 107-09

    as one religion among many, 23, 123

    and public life, 19-20, 28-32, 138-142, 147, 149, 156, 161-66

    see also Jesus Christ; Kingdom of Christ

Christian nation (three definitions), 31-34

Christian political party, 153-55

Christian school movement, 141

Christian world view, 85

    Earth as God's creation, 39-41, 70-73, 85-88, 97

    humanity, 87

    nations, 70-73, 88, 149

    political and social, 78-81, 88-89

    social concerns, 31, 88-92, 141, 145, 147-48, 154

Church/state relations, 16, 116-17

    early Christians, 102-11

    Reformation, 111-15

Clark, Joe, 147

Conservative Protestants see Evangelical

    Protestants

Constantine, 32, 99, 108-10, 152

Conversion, 25, 73-74, 88

Corporate Christianity, 32-33

Covenant

    with Abraham, 38, 44-46

    with Moses, 47-49

Covey, Stephen R, 159

Creation, 20, 79, 85-86

Cultural pluralism, see Pluralism

D
Darby, John, 29
Darwin, Charles, 19-20, 24
David, the king, 49-55
Decalogue see Ten Commandments

E
Early Christians, 102-111
Earth as God's creation, 20, 79, 85-86
Economic situation
    in God's plan, 42-43, 52-53, 57
    moral obligations, 42-43
    problems, 42
    see also Consumerism; Social Gospel
Education, church's role,
    higher education, 153
    private Christian schools, 153
Engaging the world effectively, 140-43
"Epistle to Diognetus," 104
Eschaton (return of Christ), 83, 87, 116
Eternity,
    and time, 79, 87, 97
Ethics see Morality
Evangelical Protestants,
    new groups in 20th century, 23, 25, 28, 134-35, 140-42
    sectarianism of, 28-31, 142
    and secularization, 27-28
Evil
    defeated by Christ, 18
    entry into Earthly life see Fall
    see also Satan
Evolution, theory of, 19-21, 132

F
Fall, 41, 86
First peoples see Native peoples
Freedom
    religious liberty, 31-32
    in theory of liberalism, 25-26
Frum, Barbara, 160

as a task of government, 144-49
teachings of Jesus, 67-81
Mouw, Richard, 90

N
Nation
    building a vision, 44-47, 52-54, 88-89
    Christian meaning, 85-88, 143-151
    Old Testament vision, 44-47, 52-53, 70-73, 148-51
    tasks of a nation, 52-53
    see also Kingdom of Christ
Nationalism, 88-92, 92-95
Nation of Israel,
    chosen people, 44
    a light to the nations, 39, 92-95
Native peoples, 127
Niebuhr, H. Richard, 138, 146
Newbigin, Lesslie, 123, 125-27, 131-32
New Testament insights,
    see also Jesus Christ; Kingdom of Christ
Nicene Council, 108
Niemöller, Martin, 35, 134
Ninety-five Theses (Luther), 108
Nouwen, Henri, 160

O
O'Hair, Madalyn, 162
Okumu, Washington, 139
Old Testament vision, 38-43, 40-43, 44-47
    covenant with Abraham, 44-47, 93-94
    Davidic kingdom, 49-51, 54-59
    the economy, 57
    Fall, 41-44
    lessons for us today, 59-60
    Moses, 48-50, 143, 154, 168
    prophets, 54-55, 145
    Ten Commandments, 47-49
Organization by Christians, 140-141

U
United States,
    "manifest destiny," 95

W
Wilberforce, William, 34
Work as God's gift, 42, 86
Worldliness, 95-98
World view see Christian world view
Wright, Christopher J.W., 42

Y
Yoder, John Howard, 141-42

Z
Zealots, 63
Zwingli, Ulrich, 33

Printed in the United States
40914LVS00002B/183

9 781894 860048